ANGELS AND DEMONS:

A Patristic Perspective

ANGELS AND DEMONS:

A Patristic Perspective

HARRY BOOSALIS

ST. TIKHON'S MONASTERY PRESS
SOUTH CANAAN, PENNSYLVANIA 18459
2016

ANGELS AND DEMONS:
A Patristic Perspective

Cover Design by Fr. Joel Wilson

Published by:
St. Tikhon's Monastery Press
175 St. Tikhon's Road
Waymart, Pennsylvania 18472
USA

Printed in the United States of America

ISBN – 978-0-9974718-0-9

For my parents

Michael C. and Stella Boosalis

TABLE OF CONTENTS

ABOUT THE AUTHOR

Dr. Harry Boosalis, Th. D., graduated from Holy Cross Greek Orthodox School of Theology (Master of Divinity degree, Class of 1985) and received his doctoral degree in Orthodox Theology from the University of Thessaloniki under the direction of Professor Georgios Mantzaridis. He has been teaching Dogmatic Theology at St. Tikhon's Orthodox Seminary since the Fall of 1992. His other books include *Orthodox Spiritual Life*, *The Joy of the Holy*, *Knowledge of God*, *Taught by God* and *Holy Tradition*, all published by St. Tikhon's Monastery Press.

PREFACE

This study is comprised of three lectures in Orthodox theology, focusing on the topics of Angels, Demons and the Enigma of Evil. Although intended for first year students in the Master of Divinity program at St. Tikhon's Orthodox Seminary, its introductory level of approach makes it appealing to non-specialists as well.

Written in a reader-friendly style with a deliberate attempt at presenting the spiritual themes of Orthodox theology in a clear and coherent way, this book will benefit anyone, regardless of background, who is interested in Eastern Christian theology and spirituality.

Thoroughly founded on Holy Scripture and patristic teaching, this book is original in that it is written for seminarians preparing for ordained ministry as parish priests. It preserves its teaching purpose by retaining a practical approach and appropriate level of language.

ANGELS AND DEMONS: A Patristic Perspective is ideal for any layman who seeks to introduce himself to, or increase his knowledge of, the Eastern approach to spiritual life and the study of Orthodox theology.

Chapter One: Holy Angels

Introduction

It is interesting to observe that within the spiritual outlook of many today, there is a tendency of two extremes—both with negative results. On the one hand there is increased interest in spirituality. This includes an anxious search for spiritual experiences, acceptance of a vast world inhabited by spiritual beings and the attempt to communicate with these 'beings'. For example, Far Eastern religions, psychic phenomena, pseudo-Christian cults, neo-pagan rituals, occult practices, and witchcraft[1] are all rising in popularity, to name a few. These movements attest to the increasing spiritual thirst of modern man.

On the other hand, with man's increased dependency on science and technology, there is also a growing disregard and outright disdain for belief in the spiritual world. The initial inclination of many is not only to deny but also to discredit the existence of anything not explained through empirical evidence and scientific logic. Such skepticism also pertains to holy angels, who are often considered as mythical creatures of folklore from an outdated age.

---

[1] Of particular interest is the growth of the neo-pagan witchcraft religion known as Wicca, now listed in the 'Religious Tolerance' section of the *Chaplain's Handbook* of the US Army.

The existence of angelic beings is a matter of belief. Indeed, it is a basic element of the Orthodox Faith. Every time the Nicene Creed is recited, the Orthodox proclaim their belief in the invisible angelic world: "I believe in One God, Father All-mighty, Maker of all things, visible and invisible..."

The word 'angel' comes from the Greek ὁ ἄγγελος which means messenger.[2] Scriptural texts referring to angels are numerous. They are mentioned frequently in both Old and New Testaments. Angels are often portrayed as intermediaries between God and mankind, sent by God for specific missions, to protect someone or deliver a particular message.

Christ Himself refers repeatedly to angelic beings. They were present with Him at the most significant moments throughout His earthly life—including His birth, temptation in the desert and agony in the Garden of Gethsemane. And they will also accompany Him at His Second Coming. Angels thus played very important roles within the life of our Lord, from His conception within the Virgin's womb to His Resurrection from the empty tomb. Indeed, it was an angel who first proclaimed the wondrous words, "He is risen."[3]

---

[2] *A Patristic Greek Lexicon*, ed. G. Lampe, Oxford, 1961, p. 9.
[3] Matt. 28. 6 (NKJ). All Scriptural references are from the New King James translation unless otherwise noted.

The Apostle Paul distinguishes different types or orders of angelic beings: "For by Him all things were created that are in heaven and that are on earth, visible and invisible, whether Thrones or Dominions or Principalities or Powers. All things were created through Him and for Him."[4]

Interestingly, the Apostle also warns against the danger of worshipping angels, as occurred in some ancient heretical groups: "Let no one cheat you of your reward, taking delight in false humility and worship of angels."[5]

Before proceeding, it would be helpful to identify basic theological distinctions made by Church Fathers that are fundamental to their teachings on angels. The first distinction is between uncreated nature and created nature.[6] Uncreated nature pertains only to God. This includes the divine Persons of the Father, Son and Holy Spirit, as well as the divine essence and divine energies of God.[7] Anything existing outside of uncreated divine nature is created—created by God out of nothing.

---

[4] Col. 1. 16. Cf. Eph. 1. 21, 3. 10.
[5] Col. 2. 18.
[6] E. g., St. John Damascene, *Exact Exposition* 1. 3.
[7] "Three realities pertain to God: essence, energy and the triad of divine hypostases [persons]." St. Gregory Palamas, *Natural Chapters* 75; Συγγράμματα vol. 5, ed. P. Chrestou, Thessaloniki, 1992, p. 77, trans. Palmer, et al., in *The Philokalia*, vol. 4, London, 1995, p. 380.

Within created nature, the Church Fathers further distinguish between that which is visible and that which is invisible. Invisible created nature pertains to the angelic world. This includes not only holy angels but also the fallen angels, or demons. God did not create demons *per se*. He originally created them good and holy, but they freely chose to separate themselves from God. They became demons by their free will.

Visible created nature pertains to material creation —the entire physical universe, including mankind. In fact, man is the centerpiece of God's creation. Only man straddles both the visible and invisible aspects of creation, the material and immaterial, the physical and spiritual. Man is visible on account of his material body. Yet there is also an invisible element of human nature —the human soul.

Therefore, according to Orthodox theology, angelic nature, while created, is invisible. Human nature however, while also created, is uniquely visible as well as invisible. Man, by nature, participates in both the invisible and the visible worlds. This exalts our human nature to a very precious position within all of God's created cosmos.

The Celestial Hierarchy
of St. Dionysios the Areopagite

Interestingly, the Orthodox Church "has never had a universally accepted system or description of the angelic world, with the exception of the *Celestial Hierarchy* of pseudo-Dionysios, in which each of the nine orders of angels is considered as an intermediary between the highest power above it and the form of existence below."[8] Although the Dionysian description of angelic beings was widely accepted and highly influential, still it did not supersede the more traditional accounts found within Scripture and the liturgical life of the Church.[9]

For example, the Dionysian model gives a rather limited status to Archangels, who are assigned the second lowest level within his overall hierarchy. However, in Holy Scripture, Archangels Michael and Gabriel are the most significant and greatest leaders of the entire heavenly host.[10]

---

[8] J. Meyendorff, *Byzantine Theology*, New York, 1974, p. 136.

[9] Cf. Jaroslav Pelikan, "The doctrine of angels is a preeminent example of liturgical doctrine; for the icons and the liturgy were far more explicit in describing the angels ... than the dogma of the Church ever became ..." *The Spirit of Eastern Christendom*, Chicago, 1974, p. 142.

[10] Holy Tradition considers Michael as the Angel of Righteousness, since in Scripture he is often sent to deliver the judgments of God's righteousness, whereas Gabriel is regarded as the Angel of Mercy, sent to mankind to announce God's great love and mercy. See *The Synaxarion*, vol. 2, Ormylia, 1999, pp. 67-70.

Also, in most Orthodox churches, it is the icons of the two chief Archangels that adorn each end of the iconostasis, not those of a Seraphim or Cherubim. Therefore, it is the Liturgy "which should be considered as the main and most reliable source"[11] of Orthodox angelology. Included in this is the Church's hymnographical teachings as well. Still, it is sometimes frustrating that we know so little about these angelic beings, especially in regard to their origin and unique nature.

St. Dionysios combines the angelic orders referred to in the letters of St. Paul[12] together with the Seraphim mentioned in Isaiah[13] and the Cherubim described in Ezekiel.[14] He also adds the order of Archangels, mentioned throughout Scripture, as well as a last order referred to simply as 'Angels'.

According to Dionysios, the nine orders of angelic beings are distinguished into three different hierarchies, each consisting of three specific orders. The first are the Seraphim, Cherubim and Thrones. The second are the Dominions, Powers and Authorities. And the third are the Principalities, Archangels and Angels.

The term 'angels', then, depending on context, can refer to all the angelic beings as a whole, that is to say, all the bodiless powers—the entire heavenly host in general. Or, on the other hand, 'angels' may also refer more

---

[11] J. Meyendorff, *Byzantine Theology*, p. 136.
[12] Cf. Eph. 1. 21, 3. 10 and Col. 1. 16.
[13] See Is. 6. 2.
[14] See Ez. 1.

specifically to the last order of angelic beings within the Dionysian hierarchy, the particular order of Angels.

St. Dionysios describes the corresponding proximity of each order to God. In relation to the first hierarchy, "This first of the hierarchies ... possesses the highest order as God's immediate neighbor, being grounded directly around God ... [they] have their place beside the Godhead to whom they owe their being. They are, as it were, in the anteroom of divinity."[15]

He also provides etymological descriptions of the meaning of each order's name, conveying the different ways each imitates and conforms to God. In regard to the names of the first two orders he writes: "Those with a knowledge of Hebrew are aware of the fact that the holy name 'seraphim' means 'fire-makers', that is to say, 'carriers of warmth'. The name 'cherubim' means 'fullness of knowledge' or 'outpouring of wisdom' ... These names indicate their similarity to what God is."[16]

---

[15] St. Dionysios, *Celestial Hierarchy* 7. 2; PG 3, 205B and 208A, trans. C. Luibheid, New York, 1987, pp. 161 and 163.
[16] Ibid., 7. 1; PG 3, 205B, pp. 161-162. For further descriptions of the remaining orders see *Celestial Hierarchy* 7-9.

St. Dionysios emphasizes that each order of angels passes their particular experiences of God to the order below it.[17] The last order of angelic beings, angels *per se*, is closest to man: "For being closer to us, they, more appropriately than the previous ones, are named 'angels' insofar as their hierarchy is more concerned with revelation and is closer to the world."[18]

St. Maximos the Confessor likewise teaches that the higher orders transmit their experiences of God to the lower ones. He describes further how the last order of angels transmit their virtues and knowledge to man:

> In communicating illumination to each other, the angelic powers also communicate either their virtue or their knowledge to human nature. As regards their virtue, they communicate a goodness which imitates the goodness of God, and through this goodness they confer blessings on themselves, on one another and on their inferiors ... making them like God."[19]

---

[17] See *Celestial Hierarchy* 3. 2 and 10. 2-3; PG 3, 165AC and 273AC. Cf. St. John Damascene, "They illuminate one another by the excellence of their rank or nature. Moreover, it is evident that the more excellent communicate their brightness and their knowledge to them that are inferior." *Exact Exposition* 2. 3; PG 94, 872A, trans. F. Chase, Washington, D.C., 1958, p. 207.

[18] St. Dionysios, *Celestial Hierarchy* 9. 2; PG 3, 260A, p. 170.

[19] St. Maximos, *Four Hundred Texts on Love* 3. 33; PG 90,1028B, trans. Palmer, et al., in *The Philokalia*, vol. 2, London, 1981, p. 88. Cf. St. Dionysios, "This first group is particularly worthy of communing with God and of sharing in his work. It imitates, as far as possible, the beauty of God's condition and activity. Knowing many divine things in so superior a fashion it can have a proper share of

The Dionysian numbering of three hierarchies with three orders each conveys the belief that there is an innumerable number of angelic beings, whose actual number is beyond the abilities of human understanding: "I think we also ought to reflect on the tradition in scripture that the angels number a thousand times a thousand and ten thousand times ten thousand. These numbers, enormous to us, square and multiply themselves and thereby indicate clearly that the ranks of the heavenly beings are innumerable. So numerous indeed are the blessed armies of transcendent intelligent beings that they surpass the frail and limited realm of our physical numbers."[20]

Angelic beings infinitely outnumber human beings. In the eyes of God, the final number of human beings is actually dwarfed in comparison. St. Cyril of Jerusalem, commenting on the Parable of the Lost Sheep, refers to the one sheep as representing the finite number of mankind, whereas the ninety-nine symbolize the infinite number of angels.[21]

---

the divine knowledge and understanding. Hence, theology has transmitted to the men of earth those hymns sung by the first ranks of the angels whose gloriously transcendent enlightenment is thereby made manifest." *Celestial Hierarchy* 7. 4; PG 3, 212A, p. 165.

[20] Ibid., 14. 1; PG 3, 321A, p. 181. Cf. Rev. 5. 11 and Dan. 7. 10.

[21] See St. Cyril of Jerusalem, *Catechetical Homilies* 15. 24. He further writes, "Behold, O man, before what multitudes thou shalt come to judgment. Every race of mankind will then be present. ... Reckon all from Adam to this day. Great indeed is the multitude; but yet it is little, for the Angels are many more." Ibid., PG 33, 904AB, trans. E. Gifford, Grand Rapids, 1989, pp. 111-112.

He also adds, "The whole earth is but as a point in the midst of the one heaven and yet contains so great a multitude; what a multitude must the heaven which encircles it contain? And must not the heaven of heavens contain unimaginable numbers?"[22]

On a purely cosmic level, we see how very unique and precious it is to be human. It is only mankind—and not the angels—who are created in the image of God.[23] Furthermore, in the Person of Christ, God assumed our *human* nature and not the nature of an angelic order: "God became *man*, so that man may be made divine."[24] This is why angels serve us. This is why the devil hates us.

According to St. Gregory Palamas, "Although the angels are superior to us in many ways, yet in some respects—as we have said and as we will repeat—they fall short of us with regard to being in the image of the Creator; for we, rather than they, have been created in God's image."[25]

---

[22] St. Cyril of Jerusalem, *Catechetical Homilies* 15. 24; PG 33, 904B, trans. p. 112.

[23] Cf. Gen. 1. 26, 27, "Then God said, "Let Us make man in Our image, according to Our likeness ... So God created man in His own image; in the image of God He created him; male and female He created them."

[24] St. Athanasius the Great, *On the Incarnation* 54; PG 25, 192B [italics mine].

[25] St. Gregory Palamas, *Natural Chapters* 43; Συγγράμματα vol. 5, p. 60, trans. *The Philokalia*, vol. 4, p. 366. Cf. ibid., 62 and 63.

However, in the context of our fallen condition, he adds, "Even though we still bear God's image to a greater degree than the angels, yet as regards the likeness of God we fall far short of them."[26]

Angelic Time

When discussing the nature of angelic beings, it must be kept in mind that they do not exist in the same type of time as we do. In patristic teaching, there are three distinct modes of time.[27] We will refer to them as *eternity*, *angelic time* and *temporal time*.[28] Eternity pertains to the uncreated nature of God, angelic time to the created invisible nature of angels, and temporal time to the created visible world of man and the material universe.

Eternity is basically a mode of being where our concept of time does not apply. It is unique to God alone— to the Father, Son and Holy Spirit. Eternity doesn't mean simply endless time or time without end. It also implies no beginning.

---

[26] St. Gregory Palamas, *Natural Chapters* 64, Συγγράμματα vol. 5, p. 72, trans. *The Philokalia*, vol. 4, p. 376.
[27] Cf. Mantzaridis, *Time and Man*, South Canaan, 1996, pp. 5-10.
[28] In translation from the original Greek to English, some versions vary in regard to use of English terms, although the distinction in meaning remains the same.

In eternity there is no past, nor any future. Perhaps from the limited perspective of our temporal time, and due to constrictions of our created human language, we might say eternity is a constant 'present'.

Temporal time commences with the creation of our material universe. It has a definite beginning. It will also have a definite end. Temporal time is characterized by past, present and future.[29] The present moment constantly 'moves' and instantly becomes the past. Temporal time is thus measured by intervals of chronological duration and characterized by constant change and movement through space.[30] The present moment instantly becomes the past. Everything is constantly changing. Time flies.

It is within temporal time where man exercises his unique gift of God-given freedom. Man must freely choose to either direct himself toward his Creator, or if he so chooses, he can separate himself from Him, the Source of Life. Only mankind enjoys this unique gift of freedom.

---

[29] Cf. St. Basil the Great, "Is this not the nature of time, whose past has vanished, whose future is not yet at hand, and whose present escapes perception before it is known?" *Hexameron* 1. 5; PG 29, 13B, trans. A. Way, Washington, D. C., 1963, p. 9.
[30] Cf. St. Maximos, *Ambigua* 10; PG 91, 1164BC. Elsewhere he adds, "Time is circumscribed movement. It follows that the movement of living things within time is subject to change." *Various Texts on Theology* 5. 47; PG 90, 1368C, trans. *The Philokalia* 2, p. 272.

Indeed man must constantly choose. Our temporal time serves as the environment in which human freedom either flourishes, or becomes enslaved.

Temporal time affords mankind another unique opportunity—the opportunity to repent from our sins and wrong choices. Only man has the ability to change the way he lives. Each and every new day has the potential to mark a brand new beginning.

However, there will be a last interval of our temporal time. There will be a last year, a last month, a last week. There will be a final and 'last day'[31] when time as we know it will cease. This is why our time—why our every day—is so very precious and unique.[32]

Furthermore, eternity has entered temporal time now that God has become man. The eternal and uncreated God has bridged His eternal Kingdom with the temporal world when He assumed our created human nature and became man in the Person of Christ. By virtue of the Incarnation of the Son of God, man—through his personal participation within the ascetical, liturgical and sacramental life of Christ's Holy Church—can experience a foretaste of the grace and great glory of the eternal Kingdom of God even now, while in this temporal life.

---

[31] Cf. Matt. 24. 36; John 6. 39 and 12. 48.

[32] "This life has been given to you for repentance; do not waste it in vain pursuits." St. Isaac the Syrian, *Ascetical Homilies* 74, trans. Holy Transfiguration Monastery, Brookline, 1984, p. 364.

There is also a third type of time, which is distinct from both the eternal Kingdom of God and the temporal world of man. We will define it as 'angelic' time. Angelic time commences with the creation of the spiritual world of angelic beings. Even though they are created, angelic beings are invisible and immaterial. They do not have a physical nature as we have.

Angels are not encumbered with physical and material bodies. They are not limited by the constraints of time and place. Angelic time cannot be characterized in terms of motion and duration. It can't be compared with our time-space continuum. The angels are ageless. They know neither youth nor old age as we do.[33]

Like temporal time, angelic time also has a beginning, since angelic beings were created out of nothing (*ex nihilo*), like all else created by God. Several Church Fathers teach that the angelic world was created before the material world.[34]

---

[33] See St. Basil, "Angels do not admit any change. No one among them is a child, nor a young man, nor an old man, but in whatever state they were created in the beginning, in that state they remain ..." *Homilies on Psalms* 17. 1; PG 29, 388C, trans. A. Way, Washington, D. C., 1963, p. 276.

[34] This teaching is based on the Book of Job, where God reminds Job of His ultimate omnipotence and asks, "Where were you when I laid the foundations of the earth? ...When the stars were made and all My angels praised Me in a loud voice?" Job 38. 4-7 (LXX- SAAS). Cf. St. Basil, "This was a certain condition older than the birth of the world and proper to the supramundane powers, one beyond time ..." *Hexameron* 1. 5; PG 29, 13A, p. 9. Cf. St. John Damascene, *Exact Exposition* 2. 3.

The precise instant when angels were first created is obviously unknown to man. But it must have occurred outside our temporal time, since temporal time began only with the creation of the material and visible world. As created human beings of the visible and material order, we cannot grasp the nature of the immaterial angelic world. Nor can we fathom the type of 'time' natural to it.[35]

Appearances of Angels

From a human perspective, angels are immaterial and bodiless beings. Although they may at times appear visibly to man with seemingly corporeal bodies, this is only a result of their temporarily assuming an apparently material form, and only for a specific purpose.[36] This temporary corporeal or 'physical' form is unique to them alone. St. John Damascene teaches, "Since they are intellects [νόες], they are in places intellectually and are not corporeally circumscribed. For by nature they do not have bodily shape and they are not extended in three dimensions; rather, they are present and act in space intellectually [νοητῶς] in whatsoever place they are commanded to do so."[37]

---

[35] "In fact, there did exist something, as it seems, even before this world, which our mind can attain by contemplation, but which has been left uninvestigated because it is not adapted to those who are beginners and as yet infants in understanding." St. Basil the Great, *Hexameron* 1. 5; PG 29, 13A, pp. 8-9.

[36] "When they are seen by those who are worthy, they assume an appropriate physical form." St. Basil, *On the Holy Spirit* 16. 38; PG 32, 137A, trans. D. Anderson, Crestwood, 1980, p. 63.

[37] St. John Damascene, *Exact Exposition* 2. 3; PG 94, 869B, p. 207.

Elsewhere he explains:

> Although the angel is not contained physically
> in a place so as to assume a concrete form and
> shape, he is said to be in a place because of his
> being spiritually present there and acting ac-
> cording to his nature, and because of his being
> nowhere else but remaining spiritually circum-
> scribed there where he acts.[38]

The vision of an angel in all fullness of his natural
brilliance would terrify most human beings. When commanded to appear before man, the full extent of their
glory must be concealed: "They do not appear exactly
as they are to the just and to them that God wills them to
appear to. On the contrary, they appear under such a different form as can be seen by those who behold them."[39]

The language used by St. John Damascene as he describes the unique 'movement' of angels is interesting.
The angels are said to move very 'swiftly' or 'quickly':
"For the angel acts in different places by virtue of a natural swiftness and his ability to pass without delay, that
is swiftly, from place to place."[40] He adds, "They are vig-
orous and prompt in the execution of the divine will and
by a natural quickness they appear immediately in whatever place the divine pleasure may command."[41]

---

[38] St. John Damascene, *Exact Exposition* 1. 13; PG 94, 852C-853A,
p. 198.
[39] Ibid., 2. 3; PG 94, 869AB, p. 206.
[40] Ibid., 1. 13; PG 94, 853A, p. 198.
[41] Ibid., 2. 3; PG 94, 869C, p. 207.

Angelic Bodies

Although angels are able to transport themselves in a supernatural way from place to place, they cannot be in more than one place at one time.[42] Although they are invisible, they are not omnipresent. Only God is omnipresent. Angels are unable to act or be present in two different places at once: "The angels are circumscribed, because when they are in heaven they are not on earth, and when they are sent to earth by God they do not remain in heaven. However, they are not confined by walls or doors or bars or seals, because they are unbounded."[43]

Though not restricted by physical laws of space and time, there are still limits to where angels are present and active.

While most often referred to as 'bodiless powers', angelic beings are also referred to as having 'aerial bodies'. In comparison with man, angelic beings are considered bodiless. However, in comparison with God, neither are they purely spirit, for only God is pure spirit.

---

[42] Cf. St. John Damascene, *Exact Exposition* 1. 13.
[43] Ibid., 2. 3; PG 94, 869A, p.206. See St. Basil, "We believe that the Spirit is present everywhere, while the rest of the bodiless powers are circumscribed by place. The angel who came to Cornelius (Acts 10. 3) was not with Philip at that same time (Acts 8. 26), nor did the angel who spoke with Zechariah from the right side of the altar (Luke 1. 11) simultaneously occupy his place in heaven." *On the Holy Spirit* 23. 54; PG 32, 168C, p. 85.

St. John Damascene provides a classic definition: "Compared with us, the angel is said to be incorporeal and immaterial, although in comparison with God, Who alone is incomparable, everything proves to be gross and material, for only the Divinity is truly immaterial and incorporeal."[44] Thus, any reference to aerial bodies of angels must not be thought of in terms of materiality or physicality.

Angelic Nature

Since angels are not burdened with the weight of a material body nor constrained by limits of a biological brain, one might wonder how angels think and communicate. They obviously do not communicate the same way as you or I. Rather than try to describe how angels do in fact communicate with one another, St. John Damascene states simply how they do not: "They have no need of tongue and hearing; rather, they communicate their individual thoughts and designs to one another without having recourse to the spoken word."[45]

St. Dionysios describes the workings of the angelic mind in similar terms:

> The angelic minds draw from Wisdom their simple and blessed conceptions. They do not draw together their knowledge of God from fragments nor from bouts of perception or of discursive reasoning. And at the same time, they are

---

[44] St. John Damascene, *Exact Exposition* 2.3; PG 94, 868A, p. 205.
[45] Ibid., 2.3; PG 94, 868B-869A, p. 206.

not limited to perception and reason. Being free from all burden of matter, they think the thoughts of the divine realm ... immaterially, and in a single act.[46]

We must also note that angels are not holy by nature. They are not divine beings. Only the Father, Son and Holy Spirit are divine by nature.

Angelic beings receive their holiness from God. St. Basil clearly makes this distinction when he defends the divinity of the Person of the Holy Spirit. He emphasizes that the Holy Spirit is divine by nature, whereas angels are holy by grace:

> The pure, spiritual, and transcendent powers are called holy, because they have received holiness from the grace of the Holy Spirit ... The angelic powers are not by their own nature holy; otherwise there would be no difference between them and the Holy Spirit. Rather, they are sanctified by the Holy Spirit in proportion to their excellence. ... Holiness is not part of their essence; it is accomplished in them through communion with the Spirit.[47]

---

[46] St. Dionysios, *The Divine Names* 7. 2; PG 3, 868B, trans. C. Luibheid, New York, 1987, p. 106.

[47] St. Basil, *On the Holy Spirit* 16. 38; PG 32, 136AD-137A, pp. 62-63. He explains elsewhere in more detail, "The angels were not created infants, then perfected by gradual exercise, and thus made worthy of the reception of the Spirit; but, in their initial formation and in the material, as it were, of their substance they had holiness laid as a foundation. Wherefore, they are turned toward evil with difficulty,

Along similar lines, neither are angels immortal by nature. Their immortality is only through grace.[48]

Furthermore, it is also important to point out angels are not omniscient or all-knowing. They do not know the future. God alone is omniscient and all-knowing: "Neither the angels of God nor the evil spirits know the future. Nevertheless, they foretell it. The angels do so when God reveals the future to them and orders them to foretell it, for which reason whatever they say happens."[49]

---

for they were immediately steeled by sanctity, as by some tempering, and possessed steadfastness in virtue by the gift of the Holy Spirit." *Homilies on Psalms* 15. 4; PG 29, 333C, trans. p. 235. Cf. St. Gregory the Theologian, *Orations* 38. 9 and 45. 5.

[48] "The angel is immortal, not by nature, but by grace." St. John Damascene, *Exact Exposition* 2. 3; PG 94, 868B, p. 206. Cf. St. Dionysios, "They are not immortal, since they do not have immortality and eternal life by themselves. This is something they have from the creative Cause which produces and preserves all life." *The Divine Names* 6. 1; PG 3, 856B, p. 103.

[49] St. John Damascene, *Exact Exposition* 2. 4; PG 94, 877A, p. 209. "It is by the grace of God that they prophesy." Ibid., 2.3; PG 94, 869B, p. 206.

Angelic Freedom

Even though angels are free, they do not exercise freedom in the same way we do within our unique dimensions of space and time. We live and move within the laws of temporal time. We are free to make different, and indeed contrary, choices every day.[50]

Holy angels, however, do not fluctuate in terms of their freedom. They do not deliberate nor waver as we do. They do not fall away from God: "It is said of angels that they do not, or, as some would have it, that they cannot fall. But men fall, yet they can quickly rise again as often as this may happen to them. Devils, and devils only, never rise once they have fallen."[51]

After their initial choice, angelic beings no longer change their freely chosen condition. They have exercised their free will. They now either follow God and continually grow in God-given holiness, or they continue in their separation from Him and their deviation from the inherent goodness of their natural condition.[52]

---

[50] "Christian life is the conjunction of two wills: the Divine, eternally one, and the human, which vacillates." Archim. Sophrony, *We Shall See Him as He Is*, trans. R. Edmonds, Essex, 1998, p. 58.

[51] St. John Climacus, *The Ladder of Divine Ascent* 4; PG 88, 696D, trans. Luibheid and Russell, New York, 1982, pp. 101-102.

[52] "This is why the angels are no longer capable of falling into sin: their unwavering attachment to God or their eternal enmity against Him having been realized instantaneously and for all the ages at the moment of their creation." Vladimir Lossky, *Mystical Theology*, Crestwood, 1976, pp. 102-103.

Angels are indeed free, but their free will, from our temporal view, has been permanently stabilized once and for all. Although free, holy angels are thus unwilling to separate themselves from God: "They keep their rank by persevering in goodness, by freely choosing to never abandon serving him, who is good by nature."[53] This freely chosen condition now remains ingrained within them.[54]

St. John Damascene compares angelic freedom to the condition of man after death.[55] When the soul is separated from the body at death, it leaves the confines of temporal time. There is no longer any opportunity to change the orientation of one's free will. We simply continue onward, in an endless 'present moment', forever tending toward whatever direction we have freely chosen —either toward God, or away from Him.

St. Gregory Palamas teaches, "Angels that have fallen have acquired a noetic volition which is perpetually evil, while the good angels possess one that is perpetually good and has no need of a bridle."[56]

---

[53] St. Basil, *On the Holy Spirit* 16. 38; PG 32, 137AB, p. 63.

[54] "Remember that the heavenly powers were established by the Spirit; this establishment means that they were disinclined to fall away from good. The Spirit enables the heavenly powers to avoid evil, and persevere in goodness." Ibid., 19. 49; PG 32, 157A, p. 77.

[55] "One should note that the fall is to the angels just what death is to men. For, just as there is no repentance for men after their death, so is there none for the angels after their fall." St. John Damascene, *Exact Exposition* 2. 4; PG 94, 877C, p. 210.

[56] St. Gregory Palamas, *Natural Chapters* 62; Συγγράμματα vol. 5, p. 71, trans. *The Philokalia*, vol. 4, p. 375.

Thus angels still maintain their freedom, yet they endure in the same steadfast state and constant condition which they originally chose.

Angelic beings have made their free choice 'once' and for all 'eternity'. There is no 'change of direction' in angelic freedom. There is no vacillation. Angels were created free to either maintain their natural attachment to their Creator, or to continually separate themselves from Him.

Their fixed attraction toward God therefore does not entail the eradication of their freedom. Rather, by divine grace, it leads to the ongoing intensification and deification of their freedom: "They cannot be moved toward evil—not because of their nature, but by grace and their diligent pursuit of the only Good."[57]

In regard to angelic freedom there is thus an essential difference between an actual change of the condition of their relationship *with* God—which is no longer possible due to the nature of angelic time; and the continual growth and eternal progress of their love and perfection *in* God—which is an experience they will always enjoy.

---

[57] St. John Damascene, *Exact Exposition* 2.3; PG 94, 872B, p. 207.

Angels and Eternal Progress

Angels do not deviate from the chosen direction of their free will. They do however continue to grow and progress along the path they have freely chosen. Angels, like mankind, were created with the innate capacity to continually progress in spiritual perfection and personal participation in the divine love, life and light of God throughout all eternity.

Spiritual perfection is not achieved in the sense of attaining some static state where growth and progress cease. Perfection is not breaking through a barrier and finally arriving at an exalted spiritual condition.[58] God is infinite and eternal. All those whom He created and gifted with innate freedom, both angelic as well as human beings, who freely strive to progress and advance toward His divine likeness, will never stop becoming—by His grace—more and more like Him.

Both the angels and saints will continually grow and progress in the likeness of God. Since God is infinite, there is no limit to the perfection in one's personal participation in His divine grace and glory.

---

[58] See St. Gregory of Nyssa, "It is therefore undoubtedly impossible to attain perfection, since ... perfection is not marked off by limits. The one limit of virtue is the absence of a limit. How then would one arrive at the sought-for boundary when he can find no boundary?" *Life of Moses*, 1. 8; PG 44, 301B, trans. Malherbe and Ferguson, New York, 1978, p. 31.

There is therefore no limit to spiritual perfection—neither for the angels, nor for the saints. According to St. John Climacus, "Love has no boundary and both in the present and in the future age we will never cease to progress in it as we add light to light ... even the angels make progress and indeed they add glory to glory and knowledge to knowledge."[59] St. Gregory of Sinai adds, "It is said that in the life to come the angels and saints shall never cease to progress in increasing their gifts, striving for greater and ever greater blessings. No slackening or change from virtue to sin is admitted in that life."[60]

No matter what level of spiritual progress we may attain, nor how many virtues we may acquire, there always awaits ever further and infinite growth—throughout all of eternity. As creatures of God, we were made for immortality and eternal life. This is the ultimate destiny of our lives as human beings. This is also the eternal destiny of the holy angels as well. The angels and saints will forever dive deeper and deeper into the infinite ocean of God's limitless love and eternal glory.[61]

---

[59] St. John Climacus, *Ladder of Divine Ascent* 26; PG 88, 1068B, p. 251. He writes elsewhere that angels "never cease to make progress in love." Ibid., 27; PG 88, 1101AB, p. 264. Cf. St. Gregory Palamas, *In Defense of the Hesychasts* 2. 3. 56.

[60] St. Gregory of Sinai, *On Commandments and Doctrines* 54; PG 150, 1253D, trans. Palmer, et al., in *The Philokalia*, vol. 4, London, 1995, p. 222.

[61] See St. Porphyrios of Kafsokalivia, "That is what preoccupies me. I try to find ways to love Christ. This love is never sated. However much you love Christ, you always think that you don't love Him and you long all the more to love Him. Without being aware of it,

Angels and Orthodox Liturgical Worship

The angels never cease in their worship of the Holy Trinity; and they are continuously commemorated and called upon to participate in the liturgical life of the Orthodox Church.

Angels are mentioned frequently throughout Orthodox worship. Before beginning the Divine Liturgy, during the Service of *Proskomide* or Preparation, a portion of the *prosphora* or Holy Bread is placed on the paten in their honor.[62] Immediately after the portion cut out in commemoration of Panayia (the Mother of God), of the nine other smaller portions, the one commemorating "the Archangels Michael and Gabriel and all the other heavenly powers" is actually placed first, before the Prophets, Apostles, Church Fathers, Martyrs and those who follow.

Other prayers during the Divine Liturgy referring directly to angels include the priestly prayer immediately before the Entrance of the Gospel,[63] the Cherubic Hymn,[64]

---

you go higher and higher!" *Wounded by Love*, trans. J. Raffan, Evia, 2005, p. 99.

[62] In the Russian tradition, the angels are not commemorated here.

[63] "O Master and Lord our God, who established the heavenly orders and hosts of angels and archangels to minister unto thy glory: Grant that the holy angels may enter with our entrance, to minister with us, and with us to glorify thy goodness." *The Orthodox Liturgy*, Oxford, 1982, p. 42.

[64] "Let us the cherubim mystically representing, and unto the life-giving Trinity the thrice-holy chant intoning, now lay aside all earthly care." Ibid., p. 59.

as well as the Prayer of the Anaphora where the priest prays, "Hosts of archangels, and tens of thousands of angels wait upon thee, the many-eyed cherubim and the six-winged seraphim that soar aloft ... And with these blessed Powers, O Sovereign Lord and friend of man, we also cry aloud and say: Holy and most holy art thou, and thine only-begotten Son, and thy Holy Spirit."[65]

Many hagiographical and ascetical writings attest to accounts of angels appearing at the holy altar during the celebration of the Divine Liturgy.[66] Especially noteworthy is the *Life of St. Nephon* of Constantiana, (an ascetic bishop commemorated December 23). It is recorded how at one Liturgy in particular he conversed with an angel who was guarding the holy altar. He also saw other angels as they were descending at specific moments, participating in the chanting, accompanying the

---

[65] Ibid., pp. 72-73. See the Anaphora of St. Basil the Great, "The fountain of holiness that enableth every creature having reason, and having understanding to serve thee and pour forth an unceasing hymn of glory, for all are thy servants: angels, archangels, thrones, dominions, principalities, powers and virtues, and the many-eyed cherubim praise thee; about thee stand the seraphim, six wings hath the one and six wings hath the other: with twain they cover their faces, and with twain they cover their feet, and with twain they do fly, crying one unto another, with continuing voice, unstilled songs of praise." Ibid., p. 121.

[66] In *The Philokalia* we read of the account of Abba Philimon, "During the service, he was full of fear when the priest intoned the words, 'Holy things to the holy'. For he used to say that the whole church was then filled with holy angels ..." *A Discourse on Abba Philimon*, trans. Palmer, et al., *The Philokalia*, vol. 2, London, 1981, p. 356.

procession of the Holy Gifts and observing the worthiness, or lack thereof, of the faithful approaching for Holy Communion. They were also present at the end of the Liturgy when the priest consumed the Holy Gifts.[67]

Another interesting description of the experience of holy angels during the Divine Liturgy is provided by the late Elder Iakovos (Tsalikis) of Evia:

> People are blind and they don't see what takes place in church during the Divine Liturgy. Once I was serving and I couldn't make the Great Entrance because of what I saw. I suddenly felt someone pushing me by my shoulder and guiding me. I thought it was the chanter. I turned around and saw a huge wing that the archangel had laid on my shoulder, and that he was guiding me to make the Great Entrance. What amazing things take place in the altar during the Divine Liturgy!… Sometimes I can't handle it, and so I pass out in a chair, and so some con-celebrators conclude that I've got something wrong with my health, but they don't realize what I see and hear."[68]

Also within the liturgical life of the Church, November 8th is celebrated as a major feast, when the Synaxis of the Leaders of the Heavenly Host, Archangels

---

[67] *Stories, Sermons and Prayers of St. Nephon: An Ascetic Bishop*, trans. J. Gentithes, Minneapolis, 1989, pp. 100-102.
[68] *Precious Vessels of the Holy Spirit*, ed. H. Middleton, Thessaloniki, 2003, pp. 96-97.

Michael and Gabriel, and all the Bodiless Powers, are specially commemorated.[69] As a main feast within the life of the Church, this Synaxis of the Archangels is celebrated with an all-night vigil, including an entrance at Vespers and a Gospel reading during Matins. Oil and wine are allowed if it falls on a fast day. Rest from work is also observed.[70]

In addition, the Orthodox Church dedicates every Monday to the commemoration of the Holy Angels.[71] Special canons are sung during Matins in their honor. The Church also celebrates Salutations and offers Supplicatory Canons to the Holy Angels. There is a beautiful Supplicatory Canon to one's Guardian Angel as well. Clearly, the Orthodox Church is conscious of the continual presence and active participation of the holy angels within her liturgical worship. The faithful constantly commemorate the angels and call upon their prayers and protection.

---

[69] Other feasts include, among others, March 26th for Archangel Gabriel, and September 6th for Archangel Michael.

[70] In liturgical terms, the original Greek word ἀργία means literally 'no work'. Basically, it is meant to be a day off work. In Byzantine times this was celebrated as a non-work day when shops, businesses and government offices were closed. In modern Greece this custom is still observed, for example, on the Monday of the Holy Spirit (the day after Pentecost), as well as the Dormition of the Theotokos, Bright Monday, the Nativity of our Lord and Theophany, to name a few, which are regarded as national holidays.

[71] Tuesdays are dedicated to St. John the Baptist, Wednesdays and Fridays to the Holy Cross, Thursdays to the Holy Apostles and St. Nicholas, and Saturdays to the Departed.

Guardian Angels

Although a main aspect of the ministry of angels is to praise, honor and glorify the Holy Trinity, another important role includes their unique function as ministers to mankind: "For although angels are superior to us in dignity, it is their task obediently to execute God's design respecting us; for they are ministers sent to serve 'those who are to be the heirs of salvation'."[72]

The ministry of guardian angels is an important element of Orthodox angelology. The belief in guardian angels is sanctioned by our Lord Himself, "Take heed that you do not despise one of these little ones, for I say to you that in heaven their angels always see the face of My Father who is in heaven."[73]

One way our guardian angels serve us is by protecting us when we travel. In the Prayer for Those Who Travel we read, "O Lord Jesus Christ our God ... We humbly pray thee, O all-holy Master, by thy grace to accompany now this thy servant. And send unto him ... a Guardian Angel, guiding, preserving and delivering him from every evil assault of enemies, both visible and invisible ..."[74]

---

[72] St. Gregory Palamas, *Natural Chapters* 43; Συγγράμματα vol. 5, p. 60, trans. from *The Philokalia*, vol. 4, p. 366. Cf. Heb. 1. 14.
[73] Matt. 18. 10.
[74] Prayer for Those Who Travel, *Service Book*, Antiochian Archdiocese, New York, 1975, p. 223.

St. Gregory of Nyssa teaches that every human being has his or her own guardian angel: "God did not disregard our fall and withhold his providence. ... he appointed an angel with an incorporeal nature to help in the life of each person ..."[75] Also in *The Philokalia*, we read, "When you close the doors of your dwelling and are alone, you should know that there is present with you the angel whom God has appointed for each man ..."[76] St. John Chrysostom also adds, "Near each one of us Angels are sitting; and yet we snore through the whole night. And would it were only this."[77]

St. Basil teaches that when we live uprightly and avoid sin, we make it easier for our guardian angel to defend and protect us.[78] However, when we sin and practice evil deeds, our angel is repulsed—repelled like bees from smoke or doves from foul odor.[79]

---

[75] St. Gregory of Nyssa, *The Life of Moses* 2. 45; PG 44, 337D, trans. Malherbe and Ferguson, New York, 1978, p. 64.

[76] St. Antony the Great, *On the Character of Men* 62; trans. *The Philokalia*, vol. 1, p. 338.

[77] St. John Chrysostom, *Homilies on Hebrews* 14. 10; PG 63, 116, trans. F. Gardiner, Grand Rapids, 1978, p. 438.

[78] See St. Basil, "If you have in your soul works worthy of angelic custody, and if a mind rich in the contemplation of truth dwells within you, because of the wealth of your esteemed works of virtue God necessarily establishes guards and custodians beside you and fortifies you with the guardianship of angels." St. Basil, *Homilies on Psalms* 16. 5; PG 29, 364B, pp. 257-258.

[79] "An angel attends everyone who believes in the Lord if we never chase him away by our evil deeds. As smoke puts the bees to flight, and a foul smell drives away the doves, so also the lamentable and foul sin keeps away the angel, the guardian of our life." Ibid., PG 29, 364B, p. 257.

As Orthodox believers, we continuously entreat the Lord that His angels may remain near us, in spite of our sins which separate us from Him. Throughout the liturgical life of the Church, the faithful call upon the Lord to provide them with the help of His holy angels.

We pray constantly that our guardian angel continue to preserve and protect us: "For an angel of peace, a faithful guide and guardian of our souls and bodies, let us entreat the Lord."[80] Particularly noteworthy are the references to guardian angels found within the Anaphora of the Liturgy of St. Basil the Great, as well as the Kneeling Prayers for the Sunday Vespers of Pentecost. At the Anaphora of St. Basil, the priest prays, "For thou, good Master, didst not wholly forsake thy creature which thou hadst made, neither didst thou forget the works of thy hands, but ... Thou didst appoint angels over us to guard us."[81] Also, at the Kneeling Prayers for the Vespers of Pentecost, during the first Prayer the priest prays, "Entrust Thy people unto a faithful Guardian Angel ...", and at the third Prayer, he prays on behalf of the departed, "Therefore, O Master, accept our prayers and supplications, and grant rest unto all ... that have gone to rest before us ... guiding them into Thy holy mansions by Thy radiant Angels ..."[82]

---

[80] See the Litany of Supplication after the Great Entrance during the Divine Liturgy, as well as before the Lord's Prayer.

[81] *The Orthodox Liturgy*, Oxford, 1982, p. 123.

[82] *The Pentecostarion*, trans. Holy Transfiguration Monastery, Brookline, 2014, pp. 421 and 425.

Also, at every Compline Service, at the end of each day, the believer recites a special prayer asking for the intercessions and protection of his Guardian Angel.

Conclusion

As we conclude, we see how the Orthodox understanding of angels is seen in light of Holy Scripture, the Church's liturgical life and the writings of the Church Fathers. Although holy angels are liturgical spirits who worship the Holy Trinity, much of their ministry is directed toward mankind.

Holy angels providentially care for us and continually protect us throughout the different stages of our life. They are always present with us in ways we cannot know. They are constantly concerned for us. They pray with us and guide us; they correct and protect us. They rejoice when we pray, pursue virtue and practice good deeds. And they sorrow over our sins and mourn when we fall. They are intimately involved in our entire life —from our birth and baptism to the very moment of our death.

Let each of us be reminded, how we are called to continually seek the intercessions and spiritual protecttion of our own personal Guardian Angel.

We close with these inspiring words taken from the prayers of the Supplicatory Canon to Our Guardian Angel:

"O divine Angel of God Almighty, I hymn thee, the unsleeping guardian of my soul, the protector of my life, and the guide given me from God."[83]

"O guardian of my soul and body, O divine and all-holy Angel appointed to me by God ... deliver me from the diverse snares of the wily one, and make the God Whom we have in common merciful that He may grant me remission at the judgment."[84]

"O minister of God, my most excellent guardian, abide forever with me the sinner, delivering me from the demons' wickedness and guiding me toward the divine paths that lead to unfading life."[85]

"O my guide and guardian, my protector and deliverer, the overseer of my desperate soul, when the trumpet's dread sound shall raise me from the earth for judgment, then gladsome and graceful stand near me, dispelling fear from me with the hope of salvation."[86]

"Thanks unto Jesus Christ, Who gave thee unto me as my soul's great, holy guardian and weapon against enemies, O Angel honored by God ... Vouchsafe that I attain also unto the Kingdom of Christ our God ."[87] *Amen.*

---

[83] Heirmos of Ode One, A Supplicatory Canon to the Guardian Angel, from *A Prayer Book for Orthodox Christians*, trans. Holy Transfiguration Monastery, Brookline, 1987, p. 303.

[84] Sessional Hymn, Fourth Tone, ibid., p. 306.

[85] Kontakion, Second Tone, ibid., p. 311.

[86] Heirmos of Ode One, ibid., p. 315.

[87] Heirmos of Ode Nine, ibid., p. 318.

Chapter Two: Demons

Introduction

In the Orthodox Church, few doctrines concerning the devil and demons are officially proclaimed dogma. Still, the Church provides fundamental teachings based on Holy Scripture and writings of the Church Fathers. In Greek, the word for the devil is ὁ διάβολος, which means slanderer.[1] Christ Himself refers to the devil as the father of lies, a murderer from the beginning, and the ruler of this world.[2] The New Testament also refers to him as the ruler of demons and the god of this age.[3]

The devil was originally created as the great and glorious Lucifer, the brilliant Morning Star and bearer of light. He was bestowed with "every virtue and all wisdom."[4] According to St. John Damascene, "he was created a shining and most bright angel by the Creator"[5] as the "chief of the terrestrial order ... entrusted by God with the custody of the earth."[6]

---

[1] *A Patristic Greek Lexicon*, ed. G. Lampe, Oxford, 1961, p. 344. Ὁ διάβολος stems from the verb διαβάλλω, which is translated as 'accuse' or 'deceive by false accounts', ibid., p. 390.
[2] See John 8. 44, 12. 3, 14. 30 and 16. 11.
[3] Cf. Matt. 12. 24 and 2 Cor. 4. 4.
[4] St. John Cassian, *On the Eight Vices*, trans. Palmer, et al., in *The Philokalia*, vol. 1, London, 1979, p. 92.
[5] St. John Damascene, *Exact Exposition* 4. 20; PG 94, 1196D, trans. F. Chase, Washington D.C., 1958, p. 387.
[6] Ibid., 2. 4; PG 94, 873C-876A, p. 209.

Sadly, Lucifer chose to become Satan: "How you are fallen from heaven, O Lucifer, who rose up in the morning! He who sends for all the nations is crushed to the earth. For you said in your mind, 'I will ascend into heaven: I will place my throne above the stars of heaven. I will sit on a lofty mountain, on the lofty mountains toward the north. I will ascend above the clouds; I will be like the Most High. But now you shall descend to Hades, to the foundations of the earth."[7]

Like all other angelic beings, Lucifer was created free to choose to pursue God and participate in His holiness. Or, if he so desired, he could misuse his freedom by choosing to alienate and distance himself from God his Creator.[8] When he chose rebellion against God, Lucifer became Satan, enslaved to his own evil will.[9]

St. Gregory Palamas writes, "His essence was capable of admitting evil since he was honored with free will. Had he voluntarily accepted a subordinate status ... he would have partaken of true life. But since he deliberately gave himself over to evil, he was deprived of true life and was justly expelled from it, having himself

---

[7] Is. 14. 12-14.

[8] "He freely departed from his natural virtue, fell into the darkness of evil, and was removed far from God, the only Good and the only Giver of life and light." St. John Damascene, *Exact Exposition* 4. 20; PG 94, 1196D, p. 387.

[9] "By his free choice he turned from what was according to nature to what was against it." Ibid., 2. 4; PG 94, 876A, p. 209.

abandoned it in the first place."[10] Satan thus became the primal source of all evil that subsequently infected God's creation.[11] And he enticed other angelic beings to follow him.

The angelic rebellion is described in the Book of Revelation: "And war broke out in heaven: Michael and his angels fought with the dragon; and the dragon and his angels fought, but they did not prevail, nor was a place found for them in heaven any longer. So the great dragon was cast out, that serpent of old, called the Devil and Satan, who deceives the whole world; he was cast to earth, and his angels were cast out with him."[12]

Holy Scripture states that a third of the angelic host fell away, becoming demons.[13] The fraction 'a third' may not imply an exact amount. Perhaps it is a way of conveying the truth that a large number of angelic beings, but clearly not the majority, fell away. The main point is that there are more good angels than demons.[14]

---

[10] St. Gregory Palamas, *Natural Chapters* 41; *Συγγράμματα* vol. 5, ed. P. Chrestou, Thessaloniki, 1992, p. 59, trans. Palmer, et al., in *The Philokalia*, vol. 4, London, 1995, p. 365.

[11] "The devil then is the first author of sin, and the father of the wicked ... none sinned before him." St. Cyril of Jerusalem, *Catechetical Lectures* 2. 4; PG 33, 412B, trans. E. Gifford, Grand Rapids, 1989, pp. 8-9.

[12] Rev. 12. 7-9.

[13] "Behold, a great, fiery red dragon having seven heads and ten horns, and seven diadems on his heads. His tail drew a third of the stars of heaven and threw them to the earth ..." Rev. 12. 3-4.

[14] Cf. *The Sayings of the Desert Fathers*, Abba Moses 1.

St. John Damascene comments on the fall of Satan:

> Although he had been made for good and had
> in himself not the slightest trace of evil from
> the Creator, he did not keep the brightness and
> dignity which the Creator had bestowed upon
> him. ... Having become stirred up against the
> God who created him and having willed to re-
> bel against Him, he was the first to abandon
> good and become evil... Together with him a
> numberless horde of the angels that he had
> marshaled were torn away, and followed after
> him and fell. Hence, although they were of the
> same nature as the angels, they have become
> bad by freely turning from good to evil.[15]

Demons were originally created good and in every
way just like all angels created by God. But like Lucifer, instead of using their God-given freedom to progress in holiness, they too chose rebellion against their
Creator: "If they are called evil it is not in respect of
their being, since they owe their origin to the Good and
were the recipients of a good being ...They are called
evil because of the deprivation, the abandonment, [and]
the rejection of the virtues ... appropriate to them."[16]

---

[15] St. John Damascene, *Exact Exposition* 2. 4; PG 94, 876AB, p. 209.

[16] St. Dionysios, *The Divine Names* 4. 23; PG 3, 725AC, trans. C.
Luibheid, New York, 1987, pp. 90-91. Cf. ibid., 4. 34. See also St.
Gregory of Nyssa, "As the end of life is the beginning of death, so
also stopping in the race of virtue marks the beginning of the race of
evil." *The Life of Moses* 1. 6; PG 44, 300D-301A, trans. Malherbe
and Ferguson, New York, 1978, p. 30.

Through the misuse of their free will they also fell.
Many good angelic beings thus became demons: "angels who did not keep their proper domain, but left their own abode."[17] Rather than living in the divine light of God, they now dwell in spiritual darkness:

> The angels are ordained to serve the Creator ...
> and their appointed role is to be ruled by God.
> ... Yet Satan presumptuously yearned to rule
> contrary to the will of the Creator, and when together with his fellow apostate angels he forsook his proper rank, he was rightly abandoned
> by the true Source of life and illumination and
> clothed himself in death and eternal darkness.[18]

---

[17] Jude 6.

[18] St. Gregory Palamas, *Natural Chapters* 44; Συγγράμματα vol. 5, p. 60, trans. *The Philokalia*, vol. 4, p. 366.

Satan's Pride

Pride preceded the fall of Lucifer.[19] Pride led Lucifer to lust for equality with God Himself.[20] St. Gregory Palamas is more specific. He attributes Lucifer's fall to his desire for equal authority with God:

> He desired in his arrogance to become like the Creator in authority; and he was justly abandoned by God to the same degree that he himself had first abandoned God. So total was his defection from God that he became His opponent and adversary and manifest enemy.[21]

Rather than being grateful to God and offering humble thankfulness for the many blessings he was given, Lucifer demanded more. He arrogantly insisted on equality with God.

---

[19] See St. Philotheos of Sinai, "Satan fell when he became proud … Through his pride he proved himself in God's sight more degraded than any other created thing." *Texts on Watchfulness* 14, trans. Palmer, et al., *The Philokalia*, vol. 3, London, 1984, p. 20.

[20] "The angel who fell from heaven because of his pride … had been created by God and adorned with every virtue and all wisdom, but he did not want to ascribe this to the grace of the Lord. He ascribed it to his own nature and as a result regarded himself as equal to God." St. John Cassian, *On the Eight Vices*, trans. *The Philokalia*, vol. 1, p. 92.

[21] St. Gregory Palamas, *Natural Chapters* 41, Συγγράμματα vol. 5, p. 58, trans. *The Philokalia*, vol. 4, p. 364.

The virtue of gratitude characterizes the pre-fallen condition of both angelic as well as human beings. It is natural for angels and humans to offer thanks to God. And we express our thankfulness *in* prayer and *through* prayer. On the other hand, ingratitude is a symptom of the Fall. Ingratitude is indicative of man's separation from God. Ingratitude is *un*-natural to both mankind and the angels.

It is interesting to compare the pride of Satan with the humility of Christ. Satan was created as one of the chief and most glorious angels of God. Yet pride and love for himself led to ungratefulness. He became dissatisfied with who he was and what he had been given. He insisted on equality between God and himself.

Christ, however, is God—the Only-begotten Son of God and Creator of the entire universe.[22] Yet on account of His humility and great love for all mankind, Christ, "who though He was in the form of God, did not count equality with God a thing to be grasped ... but emptied himself, taking the form of a servant, being born in the likeness of men."[23] Satan personifies self-interested pride and love for one's 'self'—to the exclusion of all others, including God. Whereas Christ is the personification of self-denial and self-emptying humility, to the point of all-inclusive love for all mankind.

---

[22] "For by Him all things were created that are in heaven and that are on earth. ... All things were created through Him and for Him." Col. 1. 16.

[23] Phil. 2. 6-7 (RSV).

When man's love for himself does not allow self-denial and self-emptying in love for all others, as Christ
lived and taught, then pride can transform him into a little satan.[24] Rather than becoming Christ-like, man can
become *Anti*-Christ-like. Man can become like the devil.[25]

Pride is clearly demonic: "Pride is the principle of
evil, the root of all tragedy, the sower of enmity, the de-
stroyer of peace... In pride lies the essence of hell. Pride
is the 'outer darkness' where man loses contact with the
God of love."[26] Ironically, although Satan desired equality with God, his pride in fact separated him from God.
The devil and his demons have alienated themselves
from the life and love of the Holy Trinity. Through the
passion of pride, man too becomes his own demon.[27]
Rather than fulfilling his destiny to become a 'partaker
of divine nature',[28] man partakes instead in pride and
thus separates himself from God.[29]

---

[24] St. John Climacus considers pride as a 'devilish disposition'.
The Ladder of Divine Ascent 23; PG 88, 965C, trans. Luibheid and
Russell, New York, 1982, p. 207. Conversely, Elder Sophrony refers to man's potential of becoming a 'micro-theos' or 'little god'.
See *We Shall See Him As He Is*, p. 194.
[25] Cf. Archim. Sophrony, "Through pride we become like demons."
On Prayer, trans. R. Edmonds, Essex, 1996, p. 88.
[26] Archim. Sophrony, *We Shall See Him As He Is*, trans. R. Edmonds, Essex, 1988, pp. 29-30.
[27] "A proud monk needs no demon. He has turned into one, an enemy to himself." St. John Climacus, *The Ladder of Divine Ascent* 23;
PG 88, 969B, p. 210.
[28] Cf. 2 Peter 1. 4.
[29] See Archim. Sophrony, *We Shall See Him As He Is*, p. 30 and *On
Prayer*, p. 157.

Elder Sophrony lists several symptoms he considers indicative of the illness of pride:

> Pride is the source of sin, comprising every aspect that evil can assume—conceit, ambition, indifference, cruelty, disregard of the suffering of others; ... gloom, melancholy, despair, animosity; envy, an inferiority complex, carnal desires; wearisome psychological disturbance, rebellious feelings, fear of death or, on the contrary, wanting to put an end to life ... These are the indication of demonic spirituality. But until they show up clearly, they pass unnoticed for many. ... In some people megalomania predominates, or ambition. With others, nostalgia, despair, hidden anxiety. In still others, it is envy, gloom, hatred. With many it is the desires of the flesh. But they all suffer from unbridled imagination and pride—masked, maybe, by an air of false humility.[30]

---

[30] Archim. Sophrony, *St. Silouan the Athonite*, trans. R. Edmonds, Essex, 1991, pp. 203-204.

Satan's Envy of Man

The passion of envy is especially noteworthy. Envy and pride are closely connected. Because of his pride and consequent desire for equality with God, Satan is now extremely envious of man—who is specially created in the very image and likeness of God Himself.[31]

The devil is dismayed at the thought of mankind being blessed with the same likeness which he himself demanded.[32] He is repulsed by the fact that God has assumed *human* nature in the Person of Christ, and that it is man who now has the potential to grow from the divine image into divine likeness. Interestingly, when the devil tempted Eve to disobey God, he used the words, "your eyes will be opened, and you will be like gods."[33]

That which Satan so passionately sought is now bestowed to man. When God became man in the Incarnation of the Son of God, human nature was lifted up to a new potential for deification in Christ. Through his personal participation in the ascetic, liturgical and sacramental life of Christ's Holy and Resurrected Body— man can indeed become, by divine grace, a 'partaker of divine nature'.[34]

---

[31] "Since he became a rebel, he is an enemy of God, and also an enemy of the human being who has come into existence according to the image of God. For on this account he hates humankind." St. Basil, *God is Not the Cause of Evil* 9; PG 31, 349C, trans. N. Harrison, Crestwood, 2005, p. 78. Cf. Gen. 1. 26.

[32] Cf. Is. 14. 14, "I will be like the Most High."

[33] Gen. 3. 5.

[34] See 2 Peter 1. 4.

Out of all God's great and many creatures, it is only man who partakes in the resurrected human nature of Christ. Only man receives the deifying Body and Blood of Christ in the Holy Eucharist. It is man's unique *human* nature which has been assumed by Christ, and not any other. Satan is thus even more envious and harbors furious hatred for all mankind—indeed, every man and woman.

Satan is enraged not only on account of our unique privilege and potential to become like God in Christ, but also because of our unique role in the cosmos:

> But because man was appointed not merely to be ruled by God but also to rule over all creatures upon the earth, the arch-fiend looked upon him with malicious eyes and made use of every ploy to deprive him of his dominion ... He deceitfully suggested such counsel as would abolish man's dominion. He beguiled him or, rather, persuaded him to disregard, disdain and reject, and indeed to oppose and to act contrary to the commandment and counsel given him by God. In this way he induced man to share in his apostasy, and so to share also in his state of e-ternal darkness and death.[35]

---

[35] St. Gregory Palamas, *Natural Chapters* 44; Συγγράμματα vol. 5, pp. 60-61, trans. *The Philokalia*, vol. 4, p. 366. Elsewhere he adds, "Unsated in his [Satan's] pursuit of evil and adding more and more to his wretchedness, he made himself into a death-generating spirit, eagerly drawing man into communion with his own state of death."

If Christ, as the Orthodox Church proclaims, is the *Phil-anthropos* (Φιλάνθρωπος) or 'lover of mankind',[36] then certainly Satan is the archetypal *mis-anthropos* (μισάνθρωπος) or misanthrope—the malicious hater of mankind.

Satan succeeded in infecting mankind with his own spiritual sickness of pride. Every human being is tempted and tried by this same passion: "Pride is the dark abyss into which man plunged when he fell. Heeding his own will, he became spiritually blind ... Intoxicated in paradise by the sweet poison of Luciferian self-divinization, man went mad and became the prisoner of hell."[37]

All of us experience our own taste of sin, which is self-separation from the Source of Life. Through pride, we separate ourselves from God. Whenever we seek our own selfish will apart from the will of God, we partake, to whatever degree, in the same passion that turned Lucifer into Satan.

Natural Chapters 41; Συγγράμματα vol. 5, p. 59, trans. *The Philokalia*, vol. 4, p. 365.

[36] Refer to the Dismissal Prayer from The Divine Liturgy of St. John Chrysostom.

[37] Archim. Sophrony, *We Shall See Him As He Is*, p. 30.

Demonic Power

Although the demons have fallen away from their natural virtues, they haven't completely lost their powers and capabilities innate to all angelic beings. Satan and his demons retain much of their angelic attributes and natural abilities.[38] Demons still live, act and move within the invisible world of angelic time, with an agility natural to all angelic beings. They are not restricted by the boundaries of physical bodies.

Their innate abilities are considerable and capable of exerting great influence upon mankind. Although they do not know the future, they do try to predict it, guessing what may happen. Sometimes their conjectures can even be correct. St. John Damascene warns us, "for this reason one must not believe them, even though they may often speak the truth."[39]

God does indeed allow demons to tempt and test mankind: "If God does give them permission they have strength, and [can] change and transform themselves into whatever apparent form they may desire ... all evil and the impure passions have been conceived by them

---

[38] "What has happened is that they have fallen away from the complete goodness granted them, and I would claim that the angelic gifts bestowed on them have never been changed inherently, that in fact they are brilliantly complete even if the demons themselves, through a failure of their powers to perceive the good, are not able to look upon them." St. Dionysios, *The Divine Names* 4.23; PG 3, 725C, trans. p. 91.

[39] St. John Damascene, *Exact Exposition* 2. 4; PG 94, 877A, p. 210.

and they have been permitted to visit attacks upon man. But they are unable to force anyone, for it is in our power either to accept the visitation or not."[40] God permits demons to test us so that we in fact may be strengthened and grow spiritually. In this way man is given the opportunity not only to progress in the likeness of God, but also to partake personally in the defeat of the devil's kingdom of evil.

Having forsaken God, the demons now focus on their goal of the spiritual destruction of mankind. They have turned the purpose of their existence into tempting and tormenting man, to make him suffer and lead him onto their same path of perdition, spiritual death and separation from God. Their enmity against each and every human person is immense: "Be sober and vigilant; because your adversary the devil walks about like a roaring lion, seeking whom he may devour."[41]

Fr. Florovsky provides a penetrating perspective on the paradoxical power of evil: "It is a kind of fiction, but a fiction loaded with enigmatic energy and power. Evil is active in the world, and in this actuality is real. Evil introduces new qualities into the world, as it were, adding something to the reality created by God, something not willed and not created by God, although tolerated by Him. And this innovation, in a certain sense 'non-being', is in an enigmatic fashion real and powerful."[42]

---

[40] St. John Damascene, *Exact Exposition* 2. 4; PG 94, 877AB, pp. 209-210.
[41] 1 Peter 5. 8.
[42] G. Florovsky, *Creation and Redemption*, Belmont, 1976, p. 50.

The devil's power is indeed enormous. He even directly challenges Christ Himself. At the Lord's temptation in the wilderness, Satan confronted Christ, daring Him to inappropriately display His divinity and authority as the Son of God.[43] Of course, Christ rebuffed the devil's temptations. Still, the dialogue attests to the magnitude of Satan's abilities, authority and arrogance. He declares his dominion and command over all worldly glory and power: "Then the devil, taking Him up on a high mountain, showed Him all the kingdoms of the world in a moment of time. And the devil said to Him, 'All this authority I will give You, and their glory; for this has been delivered to me, and I give it to whomever I wish.'"[44]

Interestingly, Christ does not contest his claim. Furthermore, Satan shows he knows Holy Scripture. And he uses it as well.[45]

---

[43] See Matt 4. 1-11; Luke 4. 1-13.
[44] Luke 4. 5-7.
[45] See Matt 4. 6; Luke 4. 10-11.

The Gadarene Demoniac

Nowhere in the New Testament is the power of demons over mankind more explicit than the numerous accounts of the demon-possessed. This is the clearest indication of the devil's hostile hatred of man and the absolute antagonism between his kingdom and the Kingdom of God. Throughout the public ministry of Christ, the Lord continually confronts and casts out demons from those who were possessed: "Then He healed many who were sick with various diseases, and cast out many demons."[46]

It is amazing to consider, especially in our time, how frequently Christ was called upon to cast out demons. It is mentioned quite frequently in the life of our Lord. One wonders how many cases were not recorded. The Apostles were also given the power and authority to cast out demons.[47] This is a common theme of many of the Lives of Saints as well.

One of the most revealing depictions of Christ in direct confrontation with demons is the account of the Gadarene Demoniac. The man was possessed not only by one demon, but many: "Then He asked him, 'What is your name?' And he answered, saying, 'My name is Legion; for we are many'."[48]

---

[46] Mark 1. 34. See also Matt 4. 24, 8. 16, 9. 32-33, 12. 22-28, et al.
[47] E. g., Mark 3. 15, Luke 10. 17 and Acts 16. 18.
[48] Mark 5. 9.

The demons are presented as wielding great power over this possessed man:

No one could bind him, not even with chains, because he had often been bound with shackles and chains. And the chains had been pulled apart by him, and the shackles broken in pieces; neither could anyone tame him. And always, night and day, he was in the mountains and in the tombs, crying out and cutting himself with stones.[49]

One of the more revealing aspects of this particular account is not so much the demons exercising such vast power over mankind, but rather that they recognized Christ as the Son of God: "And he cried out with a loud voice and said, 'What have I to do with You, Jesus, Son of the Most High God?"[50]

The main message from the Gadarene Demoniac account concerns not so much the extent of demonic power over mankind, but rather Christ's ultimate authority over the devil and his demons. The more important lesson reveals the *limits* to demonic power. Even though demons are at times allowed enormous power to tempt man, they have no power whatsoever over Christ. Neither can they defy Christ's authority. In fact they fear His authority: "I beg You, do not torment me!"[51]

---

[49] Mark 5. 3-5.
[50] Mark 5. 7.
[51] Luke 8. 28.

Limits of Demonic Power

The Lord places restrictions on the range of demonic power: "They have no power or strength against anyone, unless this be permitted them by the dispensation of God."[52] This is evident in the Book of Job. God must grant His permission before Satan is allowed to tempt and test Job.[53] Even though God consents to Satan's request, and grants him great leeway, still there are restrictions to what God allows. In this case, Job himself is clearly off limits: "But do not touch him."[54]

The Apostle Paul also attests to these limits set by God: "No temptation has overtaken you except such as is common to man; but God is faithful, who will not allow you to be tempted beyond what you are able, but with the temptation will also make the way of escape, that you may be able to bear it."[55]

---

[52] St. John Damascene, *Exact Exposition* 2. 4; PG 94, 877A, p. 209.
[53] "Then the Lord said to [the devil], 'Have you yet considered my servant Job, since there is none like him on the earth: a blameless, true, and God-fearing man, and one who abstains from every evil thing'? So the devil answered and said before the Lord, 'Does Job worship the Lord for no reason? ... But stretch out Your hand and touch all he has, and see if he will bless You to Your face.' Then the Lord said to the devil, 'Behold, whatever he has I give into your hand; but do not touch him.' Thus the devil went out from the Lord." Job 1. 8-12. See St. Macarios of Egypt, *The Fifty Spiritual Homilies* 26. 8.
[54] Job 1. 12.
[55] 1 Cor. 10. 13.

The Lord never allows us to be tested more than we are able to withstand. We are never tempted beyond our endurance. And with every trial, God always provides the strength to overcome it. Clearly, God sets restrictions to the range of demonic activity.

Furthermore, our Lord helps us make positive use of our spiritual trials. Through such testing, we can actually strengthen our soul and grow spiritually. Christ can utilize evil in order to guide the faithful toward further growth in divine grace. Indeed, the demons are at times allowed to test and tempt us; but they can never force us to consent to sin.

We read in the Acts of the Apostles, "We must through many tribulations enter the kingdom of God."[56] Through this constant 'testing', we are continually presented with opportunities to progress in the acquisition of spiritual virtues and in personal participation in divine grace and glory: "The Lord Himself guides with His grace them that are given over to God's will, and they bear all things with fortitude for the sake of God Whom they have so loved and with Whom they are glorified forever ..."[57]

---

[56] Acts 14. 22. "If we would obtain this kingdom we must remember that every spirit created in the Divine image will have to cross the threshold of suffering – voluntary suffering for the sake of holy love." Archim. Sophrony, *We Shall See Him As He Is*, p. 93.
[57] Archim. Sophrony, *St. Silouan the Athonite*, pp. 337-338.

We must never forget, it is the Lord Who permits trials and temptations for our spiritual growth. And it is the Lord Who ultimately delivers us from them as well. This teaching is found throughout Orthodox ascetical writings. According to St. Mark the Ascetic, "To accept an affliction for God's sake is a genuine act of holiness; for true love is tested by adversities. Do not claim to have acquired virtue unless you have suffered affliction, for without affliction virtue has not been tested."[58] St. Diadochos adds, "As wax cannot take the imprint of a seal unless it is warmed or softened thoroughly, so a man cannot receive the seal of God's holiness unless he is tested by labors and weaknesses."[59]

St. Isaac the Syrian also teaches, "It is not possible for any man to draw near to Christ without tribulation, and without afflictions his righteousness cannot be preserved unchanged."[60] St. Macarios of Egypt writes further, "The gift of the Holy Spirit which is given to the faithful soul comes forth with much contention, with much endurance, patience, trials, and testings. Through such, man's free will is put to the test by all sorts of afflictions."[61]

---

[58] St. Mark the Ascetic, *On the Spiritual Law* 65 and 66; PG 65, 913B, trans. Palmer, et al., in *The Philokalia*, vol. 1, London, 1979, p. 114.
[59] St. Diadochos of Photiki, *On Spiritual Knowledge* 94, trans. Palmer, et al., in *The Philokalia*, vol. 1, London, 1979, p. 291.
[60] St. Isaac the Syrian, *The Ascetical Homilies* 37, trans. Holy Transfiguration Monastery, Boston, 1984, p. 164.
[61] St. Macarios of Egypt, *The Fifty Spiritual Homilies* 9. 7; PG 34, 536BC, trans. G. Maloney, New York, 1992, p. 85.

Tactics of Demons: Intrusive Thoughts

The tactics of demons in their never-ending work of tempting and tormenting us are vast and numerous. Rather than tempting us with straightforward lies, demons more often than not seek to deceive us by distorting truth and presenting partial facts.[62] They are experts in deceit and deception. Demons are also masters at manipulating our thoughts, passions and weaknesses. They have been at it for thousands of years, harassing mankind from the very beginning.[63] They relentlessly attack each and every one of us, pushing each person's particular 'buttons' so as to provoke a negative response.[64]

---

[62] "Remember that demons do not automatically propose evil at the outset." St. John Climacus, *The Ladder of Divine Ascent* 26, p. 255.

[63] Cf. St. Macarios of Egypt, "If one man is with another person and knows things concerning him, and if you, twenty years old, know things concerning your neighbor, can Satan, who has been with you from your birth, not know your thoughts? ... Neither again do we maintain that the devil knows all the thoughts of a person's heart and its desires. Like a tree, it has many branches and limbs. So the soul has certain branches of thoughts and plans and Satan grasps some of them. There are other thoughts and intentions that are not grasped by Satan." *The Fifty Spiritual Homilies* 26. 9; PG 34, 680CD, p. 167.

[64] "We do not say that before he tempts he knows what man will intend to do. For the tempter tempts, but he does not know whether a person will obey him or not until one gives up his will as a slave." St. Macarios of Egypt, *The Fifty Spiritual Homilies* 26. 9; PG 34, 680C, p. 167.

Some demons even have specific tasks specializing in particular passions.[65] If they are unable to convince us to disregard the seriousness of our sins, they then try to lead us into despondency on account of them: "They say one thing to lead us into sin, another thing to overwhelm us in despair."[66]

Of their various strategies, we will briefly discuss two major tactics. To begin with, the battle against intrusive thoughts is one of the basic ways we must defend against the wiles of the enemy.[67] We are all aware of those annoying, disturbing and sinful thoughts tempting and testing us, particularly as we seek to grow spiritually. Intrusive thoughts, or λογισμοί (logismoi) in Greek, are referred to as 'inner voices' or 'suggestions' that beguile us and lure us to sin.[68]

These intrusive thoughts tempt everyone. While we cannot avoid them or constrain their coming, we can refuse to accept and entertain them. We have the power to reject these intrusive thoughts and dismiss them so they don't grow from thoughts into deeds and actions:

---

[65] E. g., St. Gregory of Sinai, *On Commandments and Doctrines* 74, in *The Philokalia*, vol. 4, p. 224 and Evagrios, *On Discrimination* 1, in *The Philokalia*, vol. 1, p. 38. This is also a recurring theme in *The Ladder of Divine Ascent*, particularly Chapter 26.

[66] St. John Climacus, *The Ladder of Divine Ascent* 15, p. 175.

[67] "The pressure exerted by intrusive thoughts is extraordinarily strong." Archim. Sophrony, *Saint Silouan the Athonite*, p. 446.

[68] See ibid.

"Just as people go in and out of a house, so may thoughts proceeding from devils come and go again if you do not accept them."[69]

If we are not watchful, we begin focusing on them. We can become preoccupied and obsessed with them, to the point where we are easily seduced by demonic deception and delusion.

Tactics of Demons: Spiritual Delusion

Another tactic of the demons is the enticement of spiritual pride—the same passion that turned the brightest angel, Lucifer, into the darkest enemy, Satan. Pride in our spiritual progress ultimately leads to delusion. Rather than focusing on our sins and shortcomings, and ultimately on the great mercy and love of God, our focus instead turns on our own 'self' and on our own spiritual accomplishments, virtues or blessings. In this fatal condition, we consider ourselves as favored by God, and even worthy of special blessings, divine visitations or dreams. We are thus easily deceived and darkened by spiritual delusion.

---

[69] *Saint Silouan the Athonite,* p. 446. Cf. St. John Cassian, "It is impossible for the mind not to be troubled by these thoughts. But if we exert ourselves it is within our power either to accept them and give them our attention, or to expel them. Their coming is not within our power to control, but their expulsion is." *On the Holy Fathers of Sketis,* trans. Palmer, et al., in *The Philokalia,* vol. 1, p. 97.

As we progress in the spiritual life, and advance in prayer and in the experience of God, we are susceptible to the suggestion that our spiritual growth is of our own doing, or perhaps of God's unique love for us. Our spiritual progress confirms our new found status. We might be duped into comparing ourselves with others and believe we are more spiritual or have attained a higher level of spiritual insight.[70] We may even assume we deserve special spiritual experiences and may even seek them out.[71] We then become much more susceptible to demonic deception and deceit. We become easy prey to the trickery of the demons. St. Paul forewarns us that demons may even appear as angels of light.[72]

Not only beginners, but even those who have made considerable spiritual progress, can fall victim to spiritual delusion. Rather than growing closer to Christ in love and true humility, we actually fall deeper into devious traps of satanic pride. We must never seek out spiritual visions or dreams, and we definitely must not believe them.[73]

---

[70] "We fall and are beguiled when we think ourselves more intelligent and more practised than others ... In my inexperience I thought this once, and suffered for it." *Saint Silouan the Athonite*, p. 444.

[71] "The conceited man ... wants to have visions, and deems himself worthy of them, and so it is easy for the enemy to delude him." Ibid., p. 445.

[72] "For Satan himself transforms himself into an angel of light." 2 Cor. 11. 14.

[73] Cf. *Saint Silouan the Athonite*, pp. 136-137. Cf. also Evagrius, "Take care that the crafty demons do not deceive you with some vision; be on your guard ..." *On Prayer* 94; PG 79, 1188BC, trans. Palmer, et al., in *The Philokalia*, vol. 1, p. 66.

In regard to such spiritual experiences, it is important to seek the guidance of a spiritual father. Without the insight and advice of one's spiritual father, there is little or no hope of overcoming the constant and lifelong bombardment of the spiritual struggle. The surest way to guard against the danger of delusion and deception is to seek the counsel of one's spiritual father, for to him is given a special grace of guidance and discernment.

Delusion and spiritual deception are among the main tactics of the devil and his demons: "We should not embark on the [spiritual] life in the hope of seeing visions clothed with form or shape; for if we do, Satan will find it easy to lead our soul astray. Our one purpose must be to reach the point when we perceive the love of God fully and consciously in our heart—that is, 'with all your heart, and with all your soul ... and with all your mind'."[74]

How does pride transform angels to demons? How does pride wield such power over rational beings? Why does pride make good people turn terribly bad? Perhaps the power of pride is stronger than we imagine. Infiltrating even unto the heights of the angelic hosts, egotistical pride remains the catalyst for man's separation from God.

---

[74] See St. Diadochos of Photiki, *On Spiritual Knowledge* 40, trans. *The Philokalia*, vol. 1, p. 265. Cf. Luke 10. 27.

Much of our spiritual struggle and ascetic effort is aimed against the passion of pride. The demons never cease in their assault. This battle is waged not so much against outside forces, but more so against the enemy lurking within. According to Elder Sophrony, "Both demonic images and those conjured up by man may acquire very considerable force, not because they are real in the ultimate sense of the word ... but in so far as the human will is drawn to and shaped by such images. But the Lord liberates him who repents from the sway of passion and imagination, and the Christian thus liberated laughs at the power of images."[75]

Nevertheless, demons are relentless. Their fall from grace leaves them with only one purpose—to separate as many human beings from Christ and His Holy Church as possible. Their method of operation is to entice every man and woman to partake in this same self-destructive passion of egotistical pride, and by extension its evil offspring—utter delusion and spiritual despair.

---

[75] Archim. Sophrony, *St. Silouan the Athonite*, p. 158.

Conclusion: Christ the Conqueror

In conclusion, we must always remember that regardless of their frightful power, demons wage a war they have already lost. Satan has no power or authority over Christ. The devil is defeated.[76] He is judged.[77] He is sentenced.[78] The demons are quite cognizant of this fact: "Have You come here to torment us before the time?"[79] Christ is victorious over the devil's kingdom of death. Christ has final and ultimate authority over the evil one.

And not only Christ, but His Apostles too are granted this same authority: "Then the seventy returned with joy, saying, 'Lord, even the demons are subject to us in Your name'. And He said to them ... 'Behold, I give you the authority to trample on serpents and scorpions, and over all the power of the enemy, and nothing shall by any means hurt you'."[80]

Christ the Conqueror has already defeated the devil. Christ has defeated death by His own death, laying siege to Satan's sovereignty: "Death is swallowed up in victory. O Death, where is your sting? O Hades, where is your victory?"[81]

---

[76] See Rev. 12. 10-12; 20. 10.
[77] See John 16. 11.
[78] See Matt. 25. 41.
[79] Matt. 8. 29.
[80] Luke 10. 17-20.
[81] 1 Cor. 15. 54-55. Cf. Hos. 13. 14.

Expecting to capture Christ, the devil loses all the hostages he once held captive. Even in death Christ remains the Conqueror: "For whilst expecting to have Him, he lost even those he had; and when that Body was nailed to the Cross, the dead arose. There death received his wound, having met his death-stroke from a dead body."[82]

Satan's fate is sealed. His power is usurped. Christ is risen from the dead. Evil, sin and death itself have all been conquered by the risen Christ.

We close with these words of the recently canonized St. Porphyrios of Kafsokalivia, who encourages us: "Fix your gaze unwaveringly upward toward Christ. Become familiar with Christ. Work with Christ. Live with Christ. Breathe with Christ. Suffer with Christ. Rejoice with Christ. Let Christ be everything for you. ... No one can deny that Christ is the fullness of life. Those who deny this truth are soul-sick. *They deny that which they are lacking.* And so the devil finds their soul empty and enters in. And just as a child is deeply traumatized if he is deprived of his father and mother in this life, so too, and much more so, is the person who is deprived of Christ."[83]

---

[82] St. John Chrysostom, *Homilies on Colossians* 6, trans. J. Broadus, Grand Rapids, 2004, p. 286.

[83] St. Porphyrios, *Wounded by Love*, trans. J. Raffan, Evia, 2005. p. 106.

Chapter Three: The Enigma of Evil

Introduction

The Oxford English Dictionary defines evil as 'the antithesis of Good', that which is 'morally depraved and wicked', as well as 'doing or tending to do harm'.[1] The existence of evil is one of the great enigmas of mankind. Throughout the centuries, Christian believers have wondered why a loving God allows so much evil, suffering and injustice in a world He created good.[2]

Most atheists argue the existence of evil 'proves' God doesn't exist—at least not the good, loving and personal God proclaimed by Christians. If God is omnipotent (all-powerful) and able to do anything He desires; if He is omniscient (all-knowing) and knows everything that will happen; and if He is benevolent and wills only what is good, why then do evil and suffering exist in the world?

---

[1] *The Oxford English Dictionary*, 2nd ed., vol. 5, Oxford, 1991, p. 471.
[2] "Then God saw everything He had made, and indeed, it was very good." Gen. 1. 31.

Why Does Evil Exist?

According to the Church Fathers, evil is not natural to God's creation. God did not create evil. St. Basil the Great teaches clearly, "Do not maintain that God is the cause of evil's existence, nor imagine evil to have a subsistence of its own. For wickedness does not subsist as if it were a living being."[3]

God foreknew that Lucifer and many other angels would misuse the life and freedom He granted them. He foreknew some would abuse these blessings by choosing to separate themselves from Him and become demons. Yet the question remains, why would such a good and loving God, Who knows everything and can do anything, create an angel like Lucifer whom He knew would become Satan?

The Church Fathers reply that if our all-loving, all-good and all-merciful God had *refrained* from creating angels, who were given free will and created truly good, yet freely *on their own* decided to deviate from God's goodness and pursue evil—if God *refrained* from creating them—evil would in fact have *triumphed* over God's goodness and love. His creation would be devoid of free will. Indeed, God's gift of freedom manifests His great goodness.

---

[3] St. Basil the Great, *God is Not the Cause of Evil* 5; PG 31, 341B, trans. N. Harrison, Crestwood, 2005, pp. 72-73.

St. John Damascene explains, "God in His goodness brings into being from nothing the things that are made, and He foreknows what they are going to be. ... Also, *being* [i.e., 'existence' or 'life' itself] comes first and, afterwards, being good or evil. However, had God kept from being made those who through His goodness were *to have* existence, but who by their own choice were *to become* evil, then evil would have prevailed over the goodness of God. Thus, all things which God makes He makes good, but each one becomes good or evil by his own choice."[4]

Lucifer's freedom to distance or separate Himself from God does not prevail over the goodness of God and His creation. God's creation remains inherently good, despite individual wrong choices.

On the other hand, if God refrained from creating Lucifer, and any other creature capable of choosing evil, *this* is precisely what *limits* God's infinite goodness. In other words, God does not create machines. His creatures are not robots. We are given freedom, and this reflects God's love. He does not force or manipulate us.

---

[4] St. John Damascene, *Exact Exposition* 4. 21; PG 94, 1197AB, trans. F. Chase, Washington, D.C., 1958, p. 387 [italics mine]. Cf. St. Basil, "The devil possesses a life endowed with self-determination, and the authority rests in himself either to remain with God or to become estranged from the good. ... Thus the devil is wicked because he possesses wickedness by free choice, not through a natural opposition to the good." *God is Not the Cause of Evil* 8; PG 31, 341D, trans. p. 76.

The existence of evil, which is the abuse of our freedom, does not and cannot impinge on the inherent goodness of God. Although He may permit His beloved creatures—if they so desire—to misuse His great gift of freedom, even so, the consequences of evil actions still do not infringe on the innate goodness of God's creation.

Evil Does Not 'Exist'

Discussion on evil inevitably leads to profound paradoxes. For instance, as we already noted, evil does not truly 'exist'. It has no independent existence of its own. Without the free consent of self-determining beings, evil would not be: "Evil subsists as soon as it is chosen; it comes into being whenever we elect it. It has no substance of its own; apart from deliberate choice evil exists nowhere."[5] It is a phenomenon that *exists* only when free-will is misused by rational beings. According to St. Gregory of Nyssa, evil has its "being in nonbeing."[6]

---

[5] St. Gregory of Nyssa, *On the Beatitudes* 5; PG 44, 1256B, trans. H. Graef, New York, 1954, p. 135.

[6] " Ἐν τῷ μὴ εἶναι τὸ εἶναι ἔχει." St. Gregory of Nyssa, *On the Soul and the Resurrection* 6; PG 46, 93B. Cf. St. Maximos, "Evil … does not possess any true existence whatsoever." *Various Texts on Theology* 3. 57; PG 90, 1285C, trans. Palmer, et. al., *The Philokalia*, vol. 2, London, 1981, p. 224.

Evil is referred to as 'anousios' (ἀνούσιος), which may be defined as 'non-existent'.[7] St. John Damascene teaches, "Evil is not some sort of a substance (οὐσία), nor yet a property of a substance, but an accident, that is to say, a [voluntary] deviation from the natural into the unnatural, which is just what sin is."[8] St. Maximos explains further, "Evil is not to be regarded as in the substance of creatures but in its mistaken and *irrational movement*."[9]

Evil is thus an imperfection and imbalance in the free choice of God's rational creatures. It is the misuse of freedom—a failure to cultivate the virtues natural to rational beings. Neither Satan nor his demons, nor any human being, is inherently evil by nature. Every creature—every nature—created by God is created good, indeed 'very good'.[10] There is, therefore, no evil nature *per se*.[11]

---

[7] See *A Patristic Greek Lexicon*, ed. Lampe, Oxford, p. 149.

[8] St. John Damascene, *Exact Exposition* 4. 20; PG 94, 1196C, trans. p. 387. Cf. St. Dionysios, "Evil has no substance (οὐσία)." *The Divine Names* 4. 31; PG3, 732C, trans. C. Luibheid, New York, 1987, p. 94.

[9] St. Maximos, *Four Hundred Texts on Love* 4. 14; PG 90, 1052A, trans. G. Berthold, New York, 1985, p. 77 [italics mine].

[10] See Gen. 1. 31.

[11] See St. Diadochos of Photiki, "Evil does not exist by nature, nor is any man 'naturally evil', for God made nothing that was not good." *On Spiritual Knowledge and Discrimination* 3; trans. Palmer, et al., *The Philokalia*, vol. 1, London, 1979, p. 253.

Rather than having a nature or substance of its own, evil is a deficiency of what is natural.[12] Demons are not evil *according* to their nature, but on account of their *abandonment* of pursuing their natural angelic virtues, which are, in fact, natural to them. Paradoxically, demons are evil not because of something *in* their nature, but rather something which is *not*.[13]

Since evil is un-natural, and something God did not create, it can never produce life, nurture growth, or give birth. Evil only defiles, corrupts and perverts that which already has life—that which already has an existence of its own: "Evil, *qua* evil, never produces being or birth. All it can do by itself is in a limited fashion to debase and to destroy the substance of things. ... Insofar as it is evil it neither is nor confers being."[14]

---

[12] See St. Dionysios, "[Evil] ... is neither in demons nor in us *qua* evil. What it is actually is a deficiency and a lack of the perfection of the inherent virtues. ... [a] deficiency of natural qualities, activities, and powers. ... [Evil] is against nature, a deficiency of what should be there in nature. Thus, there is no evil nature ..." *The Divine Names* 4. 24-26; PG 3, 728AC, trans. C. Luibheid, New York, 1987, p. 92.

[13] See St. Dionysios, "Their evil consists in the *lack of* the angelic virtues! ... Their deviation is the evil in them, their move away from what befits them. It is a privation in them, an imperfection ... Therefore, the tribe of demons is evil not because of what it is in its nature but on account of what it is *not*." Ibid., 4.23; PG 3, 725BC, trans. p. 91 [italics mine].

[14] St. Dionysios, *The Divine Names* 4. 20; PG 3, 717BC, trans. p. 86. He continues, "Evil therefore in itself has neither being, goodness, the capacity to beget, nor the ability to create things which have being ... Evil *qua* evil cannot produce and cannot sustain anything, cannot make or preserve anything." Ibid., 4. 20 and 28; PG 3, 717C and 729B, trans. pp. 86 and 93.

Fr. Georges Florovsky describes the parasitic nature of evil: "Evil never exists by itself but only inside of Goodness. Evil is a pure negation, a privation or a mutilation. ... evil is a lack, a defect. ... it never creates, but its destructive energy is enormous. Evil never ascends; it always descends. But the very debasement of being which it produces is frightening. ... Undoubtedly evil lives only through the Good which it deforms, but which it also adapts to its needs."[15]

Evil may thus be defined as the invention of rational beings freely choosing to do what is unnatural.[16] Evil is a lapse from what is natural to what is unnatural. In the words of St. Maximos the Confessor:

It is not food that is evil but gluttony, not the begetting of children but unchastity, not material things but avarice, not esteem but self-esteem. This being so, it is only the misuse of things that is evil, and such misuse occurs when the intellect [νοῦς] fails to cultivate its natural powers.[17]

---

[15] G. Florovsky, *Creation and Redemption*, Belmont, 1976, p. 84.

[16] "Evil is not a living and animated substance, but a condition of the soul which is opposed to virtue and which springs up in the slothful because of their falling away from good." St. Basil, *Hexaemeron* 2.4; PG 29,37D, trans. A. Way, Washington, D.C., 1963, p. 28.

[17] St. Maximos, *Four Hundred Texts on Love* 3.4; PG 90, 1017CD, trans. Palmer, et al., *The Philokalia*, vol. 2, London, 1981, p. 83.

All rational beings created by God are good by nature. But, if they freely choose to separate themselves from what is natural, they then become evil: "Evil as such has no being … evil has no share of being except in an admixture with the Good. … Its origin is due to a *defect* rather than to a capacity."[18]

Evil, Sin and Suffering

Any discussion of evil must mention sin, suffering and death. These elements are intimately interconnected. From the Orthodox perspective, sin is seen not so much in a legalistic sense, such as the breaking of a rule requiring atonement through penance or punishment. No, sin is a spiritual *sickness* separating us from God. And our spiritual sicknesses are often sources of our pain and suffering.

Elder Aimilianos of Mount Athos teaches, "The majority of illnesses have their causes not in the body, but in the soul. We are sick because we have sinned. And we are sick, not because God is punishing us, but because sickness and suffering are necessary for our correction, for our education and growth."[19]

---

[18] St. Dionysios, *The Divine Names* 4. 33-34; PG 3, 733AC, trans. p. 95 [italics mine].
[19] Archim. Aimilianos, *Psalms and the Life of Faith*, trans. M. Constans, Athens, 2015, p. 204.

Sin is a sickness requiring healing. Penance is not a punishment, but rather an initial attempt at spiritual therapy. Neither is death considered a punishment for sin. In the Book of Genesis, when God forbade Adam to eat of the Tree of the Knowledge of Good and Evil, He did not say, "If you eat of it, I will punish you with death." God said, "For in the day that you eat of it you shall surely die."[20] Death is not punishment for breaking God's rules. Rather, death is the natural outcome of separating ourselves from God—our Creator and the Source of all Life.

When the devil tempted Adam and Eve to eat the forbidden fruit, he used the words, "your eyes will be opened, and you will be like God."[21] After they chose to follow the way of the devil rather than God, they were no longer able to look upon the Lord with the innocence of young and naked children.[22] In their fallen and self-imposed state of separation, rather than seeing God as their good and loving Father, their eyes opened instead to their own nakedness: "and they knew that they were naked."[23]

---

[20] Gen. 2. 17.

[21] Gen. 3. 5.

[22] Cf. St. Basil, "But it was necessary that they not know their nakedness, that the mind of the human being might not turn toward the fulfillment of lesser needs, to consider clothes for himself and relief from nakedness, and through concern for the flesh be entirely dragged away from gazing intently toward God." *God is Not the Cause of Evil* 9; PG 31, 349A, trans. p. 77.

[23] Gen. 3. 7.

Adam and Eve chose to run away from God. They sought to hide and separate themselves from their Creator: "I heard Your voice in the garden, and I was afraid because I was naked; and I hid myself."[24] This is what all of us—every man and woman—continue to do when we sin. We think we can hide ourselves from Him Who sees all. When we sin, we willfully separate ourselves from the grace of God's presence.[25]

The universal experience of sin and suffering affects every member of the human race. Every human being suffers from some form of evil. Evil seems to surround us everywhere: "There is nowhere on earth, nor in the whole universe, where it is possible to avoid encounter with the devil. And if the devil controls not only our world but all the rest of creation, as 'prince of this world', wherever we happen to be 'geographically' and spiritually, he will come and put us to the test."[26]

Our own personal sins and evil deeds have cosmological consequences. Our personal sins affect not only our own individual lives and the lives of those around us—they also extend outward infecting all mankind.

---

[24] Gen. 3. 10.

[25] See St. Paisius of Mount Athos, "In the beginning, man had communion with God. Later, however, when he moved away from the Grace of God, he was like someone who used to live in a palace and then was banned from it and now views it from a distance and weeps. Just as a child suffers away from its mother, man also suffers when he is distanced from God. We are tormented. Separation from God is hell." *With Pain and Love*, Sourouti, 2006, p. 49.

[26] Archim. Sophrony, *We Shall See Him as He Is*, trans. R. Edmonds, Essex, 1998, p. 82.

St. Porphyrios writes: "Man has such powers that he can transmit good or evil to his environment. These matters are very delicate. ... We mustn't think anything evil about others. Even a simple glance or a sigh influences those around us. And even the slightest anger or indignation does harm. ... We transmit our evil in a mystical way. It is not God who provokes evil, but rather people's wickedness. ... Our own evil disposition is transmitted to the soul of the other in a mysterious way and does evil."[27]

As human beings, we are created to be high priests of God's great cosmos. Through the proper use of our God-given freedom, we are called to care for, cultivate, and to call down the Holy Spirit upon God's glorious creation, beginning with our own lives, our own minds and our own bodies. We are created to personally contribute to the sanctification of the cosmos.

However, when we sin and separate ourselves from our Creator, we instead make our own personal contribution to creation's estrangement and alienation from God. The truth is that we are all spiritually sick. We are all suffering.[28] And more often than not, our suffering is self-inflicted.

---

[27] St. Porphyrios, *Wounded by Love*, trans. J. Raffan, Evia, 2005, pp. 212-213.
[28] "All creation suffers. There is a cosmic suffering. The entire world is poisoned by evil and malevolent energies, and the entire world suffers because of it." G. Florovsky, *Creation and Redemption*, pp. 88-89.

According to St. Basil the Great, "Let each one recognize himself as the first author of the vice that is in him. ... Do not seek elsewhere their beginnings, but recognize that evil in its proper sense has taken its origin from our voluntary falls."[29]

The irony is that some of us want to remain sick. Some of us want to wallow in the suffering of our addictions and sinful passions. Some of us are quite content with being miserable. Not only do we suffer inwardly from our own self-inflicted suffering, but we also perpetrate evil outwardly on others. And at times, we are quite willing and happy to do so. Indeed the entire world is awash in self-inflicted suffering, carnal sin and sexual obsession.

As a result of man's sin and separation from God, our world is now infected with evil.[30] The world is now bound by sin, suffering, disease and delusion. The world in its fallen state has become dysfunctional. This is apparent both within society at large, and within the basic unit of society—the family, as well as within each and every human person.[31] Clearly, this is not the world as it was originally created by God.

---

[29] St. Basil, *Hexaemeron* 2. 5; PG 29, 40AB, trans. pp. 28-29.

[30] See G. Florovsky, "The unique source of evil, in the strict sense of the term, is sin, the opposition to God and the tragic separation from Him." *Creation and Redemption*, p. 84.

[31] See Rom. 7. 15.

Our abuse of our God-given freedom and our own ensuing sin and separation from God has led to cosmic suffering affecting all mankind. Every man and woman not only suffers, but also must one day die. All who are born this very day are ultimately destined to die. Evil, sin, suffering and death are all intimately intertwined.

Evil and Death

Death is the domain of Satan. His kingdom is one of death, not of life. And he knows his fleeting authority is only temporary. It will end one day. Lucifer, like all of God's creatures, was created for life, and not for death. Still, Lucifer chose to forsake true life and embrace the illusionary grandeur of separation from God:

> The evil one possesses not evil but life as his essence, and hence he lives immortally. ... But since he deliberately gave himself over to evil, he was deprived of true life and was justly expelled from it, having himself abandoned it in the first place. Thus he became a dead spirit, not in essence—since death lacks substantial reality—but through his rejection of true life.[32]

---

[32] St. Gregory Palamas, *Natural Chapters* 41; Συγγράμματα vol. 5, ed. P. Chrestou, Thessaloniki, 1992, pp. 58-59, trans. Palmer, et al., *The Philokalia*, vol. 4, London, 1995, p. 365.

All rational and free creatures, that is to say, all angelic and human beings, are created to participate freely in the divine life and love of God. While existence or life itself is given to all God's creatures, participation in His *divine* life of love is granted only to those who freely want to pursue it. God does not force Himself on any of His creatures.

Apart from the Source of Life, there is no *true* life for any angel or man. There is only existence within the laws of death:

> In her primordial and ultimate vocation, creation is destined for union with God, for communion and participation in His life. But this is not a binding necessity of creaturely nature. Of course, outside of God there is no life for creation. ... Being and [true] life do not coincide in creation. And therefore existence in death is possible.[33]

Mere existence does not equal true life. True life is the *abundant* life of personal participation in the divine life and love of Christ: "Christ is life, the source of life, the source of joy, the source of the true light, everything. Whoever loves Christ and other people truly lives life. Life without Christ is death; it is hell, not life. That is what hell is—the absence of love. Life is Christ.

---

[33] G. Florovsky, *Creation and Redemption*, p. 49.

Love is the life of Christ. Either you will be in life or in death. It's up to you to decide."[34]

Separation from God is in itself a form of spiritual death. Spiritual death, however, is not the end of existence. Rebellion, apostasy and separation from God do not lead to non-being. Fr. Florovsky writes:

> Even without realizing her true vocation, and even opposing it, thus undoing and losing herself, creation does not cease to exist. ... the power of self-annihilation is not given. Creation is indestructible—and not only that creation which is rooted in God as in the source of true being and eternal life, but also that creation which has set herself against God.[35]

---

[34] St. Porphyrios, *Wounded by Love*, p. 97. Cf. John 10.10, "I have come that they may have life, and that they may have it more abundantly." See also 2 Peter 1. 4, "Be partakers of divine nature ..."

[35] G. Florovsky, *Creation and Redemption*, p. 49.

Epilogue: The Battle Against Cosmic Evil

The existence of death and evil manifests the remarkable integrity with which God respects the freedom of His beloved creatures, both angelic as well as human. God adamantly maintains the honor of His great gift of freedom, in spite of the threat of evil's 'existence'. Our personal freedom is much more precious in God's eyes than we can imagine. God respects our freedom much more than we do ourselves.

We love to talk about freedom, and we cherish our freedom. We are willing to fight and even die to protect our freedom. Yet more often than not, we abuse our freedom. Rather than practicing *true* freedom, many of us instead become enslaved within a vast variety of evil passions and addictions that actually separate us from God and lead to spiritual death.

Freedom necessitates self-determination. God desires that we, like Himself, be free. God honors us with self-determination, "so that the good would belong to the one who chose it no less than to the one who provided its seeds."[36] God respects our self-determination, not only in regard to whether or not we choose to believe in Him, but also in regard to the degree we desire to participate and penetrate His divine life:

---

[36] St. Gregory the Theologian, *Orations* 45. 8; PG 36, 632C, trans. N. Harrison, Crestwood, 2008, p. 167.

The existence of every reasonable created being oscillates between two poles—the one,
love towards God to the point of self-hatred;
the other, love of self to hatred of God. No rea-
soning created being can escape these two
poles of attraction. Everything that happens in
our personal life is in reality our spiritual self-
determination precisely on this plane, regardless of whether we are rationally aware of it...[37]

Man is free. We are free not only to embrace God.
We are also free to sin and separate ourselves from Him.
We are free to embrace even evil itself. And many of us
do. The allure of evil is a powerful force that will continue to tempt and entice every one of us, until the day
we die.

Our personal response to evil determines our spiritual destiny. The enigma of evil is not simply an issue
of ethics or philosophy. The paradox of evil is properly
understood only from a spiritual perspective.[38]

---

[37] Archim. Sophrony, *St. Silouan the Athonite*, trans. R. Edmonds,
Essex, 1991, p. 218. He writes elsewhere, "We are faced with the
choice between 'the adoption of sons' (Gal. 4. 5) by our God and
Father, or withdrawing from Him 'into outer darkness' (cf. Matt.
22. 13). *There is no middle way.*" *We Shall See Him as He Is*, p. 110.
[38] See G. Florovsky, *Creation and Redemption*, p. 84. He adds,
"Formal analysis of evil is not enough. ... Only through spiritual effort can one understand and resolve this paradox, surmount this
scandal, and penetrate the mystery of Good and Evil." Ibid., p. 91.

Evil's only access of entry into creation is through free acts of rational and self-determining beings: "Evil is created by personal agents. Evil, in the strict sense of this word, exists only in persons or in their creations and their acts."[39]

The battle against cosmic evil takes place on a very personal level, and in a very personal place—the human heart: "Evil is real since it lives in our heart and there it operates by suggesting wicked and obscene thoughts ..."[40] Selfish pride and carnal passions are the primary means by which the evil one wages this personal war against every man and woman. And there are very real losses. By fanning the fires of fleshly desires, and our selfish obsessions for material possessions, the devil easily distracts and eventually darkens our hearts and minds. Through our passions and addictions we allow the evil one to take command of much of our precious time, energy and resources.

In reality, our enemy is not the devil. Our real enemy is in fact our *own* selves. More precisely, it is our own love for our *self*.

---

[39] Ibid., p. 87. He continues, "Physical and cosmic evil also originates from these personal acts. And that is why evil can have a power, can be active. For evil is a perverse personal activity. But this activity inevitably spreads itself to the impersonal." Ibid.

[40] St. Macarios of Egypt, *The Fifty Spiritual Homilies* 16. 6; PG 34, 617A, trans. p. 131. "The entire force of resistance to cosmic evil is concentrated in the deep heart of the Christian." Archim. Sophrony, *St. Silouan the Athonite*, p. 234.

It is that abnormal and obsessive over-attachment to one's *self* which is our true enemy. In patristic writings, this is referred to as *self-love.*[41]

The passion of self-love has corrupted each and every man and woman. All of us succumb, to one degree or another, to this same temptation. Self-love can enclose us within ourselves, leading us into direct opposition to the will of God and the needs of others. This leads to inner personal conflict regarding our self identity. It also impacts our perspective on the purpose of human life.

Our pride and lust to live for and love only our self, and our consequent refusal to deny and empty our self out of love for God and our fellow man, is what lies at the root of much of the disbelief and spiritual despair that characterizes our generation.[42] Our own personal participation in the primeval passions of pride and self-love adds to the overall sin and suffering saturating society today.

---

[41] The word in original Greek is φιλαυτία. See *A Patristic Greek Lexicon*, ed. G. Lampe, p.1476. Cf. J. Larchet, *Therapy of Spiritual Illnesses*, vol. 1, Montreal, 2012, pp. 145-150.

[42] "So long as pride is deeply rooted in him, man is subject to particularly painful, hellish despair, that distorts his every notion of God and the ways of His providence. The proud soul, plunged in the torments and shades of hell, sees God as the cause of her sufferings and considers Him immeasurably cruel. Deprived of true life in God, she sees everything through the spectrum of her own crippled state, and ... in her despair she begins to consider even the existence of God Himself as hopeless absurdity." Archim. Sophrony, *Saint Silouan the Athonite*, pp. 201-202.

We all, each and every one of us, either contribute to the cure of our common spiritual disease, or we serve as agents in spreading its contamination.

Nevertheless, God has implemented His final solution to the problem of evil. The Person of Christ has truly set us free. We are now liberated from the bonds of evil, sin, suffering and death through the Crucifixion, Death and Resurrection of our Lord and Savior Jesus Christ.

Our abuse of God's gift of freedom must not be seen in terms of a vengeful and wrathful God Who waits to chastise us for misusing it. Rather, our sin and suffering must be seen in light of the love, mercy and compassion of our personal God—the Son of God—our Lord Jesus Christ.

Christ not only patiently tolerates our abuse of our freedom and the evil which arises from it. He also co-suffers with us. Indeed, He Himself shares in our personal battles against evil, sin, suffering and death. Out of His great compassion and love for mankind, Christ takes upon Himself the sufferings of each person. In His love He suffers, with the same suffering that is in each of us.[43]

---

[43] "In taking upon himself by his own suffering the sufferings of each one ... [he suffers] mystically out of goodness in proportion to each one's suffering." St. Maximos the Confessor, *Mystagogy* 24; PG 91, 713B, trans. G. Berthold, New York, 1985, p. 212. He adds elsewhere, "If God suffers in the flesh, when He is made man, should we not rejoice when we suffer, for we have God to share our

Christ maintains the integrity of our freedom by co-suffering with us in our abuse of our freedom. He co-suffers with us in our self-inflicted sin and sufferings. Christ even dies with us, yet rises from death, breaking the bonds of death itself.

Even further, Christ empowers us, as living members of His Holy and Resurrected Body, with the means to defeat the forces of evil in our own personal lives. Through the ascetic, sacramental and liturgical life of the Church, man is led to spiritual therapy, where the illnesses of egotistical pride and self-love can be properly treated and cured: "We have it in our power either to abide in virtue and follow God, Who calls us into the ways of virtue, or to stray from the paths of virtue, which is to dwell in wickedness, and to follow the devil who summons [us] but cannot compel us."[44]

As we conclude our discussion on the battle against cosmic evil, there is one final yet fundamental point to be mentioned. In addition to our corporate participation in the life of the Church, we also have at our direct disposal the ultimate power of the Name of Jesus—the Jesus Prayer.

---

sufferings? This shared suffering confers the kingdom on us." St. Maximos the Confessor, *Various Texts on Theology* 1. 24; PG 90, 1188D-1189A, trans. *The Philokalia*, vol. 2, p. 170.

[44] St. John Damascene, *Exact Exposition* 2. 30; PG 94, 973A, trans. S. Salmond, Grand Rapids, 2004, p. 43. Cf. St. John Chrysostom, "How then, you may say, are we to wrestle with the darkness? By becoming light ... by becoming good. For wickedness is contrary to good, and light drives away darkness." *Homilies on Ephesians* 22; trans. G. Alexander, Grand Rapids, 2004, p. 161.

Christ has bequeathed to all who believe in Him immediate access to the world's greatest spiritual power against the forces of evil. As simple as it may sound, the menacing power of evil is defanged by the humble and contrite repetition of the name of the Lord Jesus Christ.

St. Porphyrios speaks from his own personal experience: "You won't become saints by hounding after evil. Ignore evil. Look towards Christ and He will save you. ... If evil comes to assault you, turn all your inner strength to good, to Christ. Pray 'Lord Jesus Christ, have mercy on me.' He knows how and in what way to have mercy on you. ... In this way you become good on your own, with the grace of God. Where can evil then find a foothold? It disappears!"[45]

The Jesus Prayer is remarkably pertinent for today. Every believer, in any situation, can call upon the power of the Name of Jesus. Accessible to all at any time and any place, the Jesus Prayer does not require any special level of spiritual experience in order to pursue its practice.

By repentantly repeating those blessed words, *Lord Jesus Christ, Son of God, have mercy on me a sinner*, we personally participate in an ancient Eastern Christian technique of prayer.

---

[45] St. Porphyrios, *Wounded by Love*, trans. J. Raffan, Evia, 2005, p. 135.

There is great and unseen spiritual power in the Name of Jesus. At the Name of Jesus, the demons flee: "Therefore God also has highly exalted Him and given Him the name which is above every name, that at the name of Jesus every knee should bow, of those in heaven, and of those on earth, and of those under the earth ..."[46]

St. John Climacus considers the Name of Jesus to be the greatest of all weapons: "Flog your enemies with the name of Jesus, since there is no stronger weapon in heaven or on earth."[47]

St. Hesychios emphasizes the effectiveness of the Jesus Prayer in the battle against intrusive thoughts: "Whenever we are filled with evil thoughts, we should throw the invocation of our Lord Jesus Christ into their midst. Then, as experience has taught us, we shall see them instantly dispersed, like smoke in the air."[48]

In closing, Elder Sophrony summarizes the Orthodox response to the threat of evil. He too stresses the role of the Jesus Prayer in evil's ultimate defeat: "The power of cosmic evil over man is colossal, and such as no son of Adam can overcome without Christ and outside Christ. He is Jesus the Savior, in the literal and sole

---

[46] Phil. 2. 9-10. Cf. Acts 4. 12. See Acts 3. 6-16, where the Apostle Peter heals the lame man through the invocation of the Name of Jesus. Cf. also Acts 9. 34.

[47] St. John Climacus, *The Ladder of Divine Ascent* 21; PG 88, 945C, trans. C. Luibheid and N. Russell, New York, 1982, p. 200.

[48] St. Hesychios, *On Watchfulness and Holiness* 98; PG 93, 1509C, trans. *The Philokalia*, vol. 1, p. 179.

sense of the word. This is the Orthodox ascetic's belief, and he therefore pursues the prayer of inner stillness by the unceasing invocation of the Name of Jesus Christ, which is why this prayer is called the Jesus Prayer."[49]

It is imperative to bear in mind that we do not encounter evil alone. We never fight evil in isolation. Christ is *always* with us—as are His holy angels and all His saints—if we so *choose*.

In those very difficult moments of our personal lives, when we may be suffering from any kind of spiritual trial, tribulation or evil temptation, the powerful peace of Christ is always close at hand.

Let us end with the words of our Lord Himself, Who encourages us all, "Peace I leave with you, My peace, I give to you; not as the world gives do I give to you. Let not your heart be troubled, neither let it be afraid."[50]

"These things I have spoken to you, that in Me you may have peace. In the world, you will have tribulation; but be of good cheer, for I have overcome the world."[51]

Amen.

---

[49] Archim. Sophrony, *St. Silouan the Athonite*, p. 159.
[50] Jn. 14. 27.
[51] Jn. 16. 33.

Select Bibliography

Patristic Writings

ATHANASIUS THE GREAT. *On the Incarnation.* Trans. C. S. M. V. Crestwood: St. Vladimir's Seminary Press, 1953.

BASIL THE GREAT. *On the Holy Spirit.* Trans. D. Anderson. Crestwood: St. Vladimir's Seminary Press, 1980.

———— *Hexaemeron.* Trans. A. C. Way. The Fathers of the Church, vol. 46. Washington, D.C: The Catholic University of America Press, 1963.

———— *Homilies on Psalms.* Trans. A. C. Way. The Fathers of the Church, vol. 46. Washington, D.C: The Catholic University of America Press, 1963.

———— *God is Not the Cause of Evil.* Trans. N. Harrison. (*On the Human Condition*). Crestwood: St. Vladimir's Seminary Press, 2005.

CYRIL OF JERUSALEM. *Catechetical Homilies.* Trans. E. Gifford. The Nicene and Post-Nicene Fathers, 2nd series, vol. 7. Grand Rapids: W. B. Eerdmans, 1989.

DIADOCHOS OF PHOTIKI. *On Spiritual Knowledge and Discrimination: 100 Texts.* Trans. Palmer, Sherrard and Ware. The Philokalia, vol. 1. London: Faber and Faber, 1979.

DIONYSIOS THE AREOPAGITE. *The Divine Names.* Trans. C. Luibheid. (*The Complete Works*). The Classics of Western Spirituality. New York: Paulist Press, 1987.

———— *The Celestial Hierarchy.* Trans. C. Luibheid. (*The Complete Works*). The Classics of Western Spirituality. New York: Paulist Press, 1987.

GREGORY OF NYSSA. *The Beatitudes.* Trans. H. Graef. Ancient Christian Writers, vol. 18. New York: Paulist Press, 1954.

———— *The Life of Moses.* Trans. A. Malherbe and E. Ferguson. The Classics of Western Spirituality. New York: Paulist Press, 1978.

———— *On the Soul and the Resurrection.* Trans. C. Roth. Crestwood: St. Vladimir's Seminary Press, 1993.

GREGORY PALAMAS. *The Natural Chapters.* Trans. Palmer, Sherrard and Ware. The Philokalia, vol. 4. London: Faber and Faber, 1995.

GREGORY OF SINAI. *On Commandments and Doctrines.* Trans. Palmer, Sherrard and Ware. The Philokalia, vol. 4. London: Faber and Faber, 1995.

GREGORY THE THEOLOGIAN. *Festal Orations*. Trans. N. Harrison. Crestwood: St. Vladimir's Seminary Press, 1977.

ISAAC THE SYRIAN. *Ascetical Homilies*. Trans. Holy Transfiguration Monastery. Brookline: Holy Transfiguration Press, 1984.

JOHN CASSIAN. *On the Eight Vices*. Trans. Palmer, Sherrard and Ware. The Philokalia, vol. 1. London: Faber and Faber, 1979.

JOHN CLIMACUS. *The Ladder of Divine Ascent*. Trans. C. Luibheid and N. Russell. The Classics of Western Spirituality. New York: Paulist Press, 1982.

JOHN DAMASCENE. *Exact Exposition of the Orthodox Faith*. Trans. F. Chase. The Fathers of the Church, vol. 37. Washington, D.C: The Catholic University of America Press, 1958.

MACARIOS OF EGYPT. *The Fifty Spiritual Homilies*. Trans. G. Maloney. The Classics of Western Spirituality. New York: Paulist Press, 1992.

MAXIMOS THE CONFESSOR. *Four Hundred Texts on Love*. Trans. Palmer, Sherrard and Ware. The Philokalia, vol. 2. London: Faber and Faber, 1981.

——— *Two Hundred Texts on Theology*. Trans. Palmer, Sherrard and Ware. The Philokalia, vol. 2. London: Faber and Faber, 1981.

Modern Authors

AIMILIANOS, ARCHIMANDRITE. *The Way of the Spirit.* Trans. M. Maximos, Athens: Indiktos, 2009.

———— *Psalms and the Life of Faith.* Trans. M. Maximos, Athens: Indiktos, 2015.

ALEXANDRA, MOTHER. *The Holy Angels.* Minneapolis: Light and Life Publishing, 1987.

BOOSALIS, HARRY. *Orthodox Spiritual Life.* South Canaan: St. Tikhon's Seminary Press, 2000.

FLOROVSKY, GEORGES. *Creation and Redemption.* Belmont: Nordland Publishing, 1976.

LOSSKY, VLADIMIR. *The Mystical Theology of the Eastern Church.* Crestwood: St. Vladimir's Seminary Press, 1976.

MANTZARIDIS, GEORGE. *Orthodox Spiritual Life.* Trans. K. Schram. Brookline: Holy Cross Press, 1994.

———— *Time and Man.* Trans. J. Vulliamy. South Canaan: St. Tikhon's Seminary Press, 1996.

MEYENDORFF, JOHN. *Byzantine Theology.* New York: Fordham University Press, 1974.

PAISIUS, SAINT. *Spiritual Struggle.* Trans. P. Chamberas. Thessaloniki: Holy Monastery of the Evangelist John the Theologian, 2010.

———— *With Pain and Love.* Trans. C. Tsakiridou and M. Spanou. Thessaloniki: Holy Monastery of the Evangelist John the Theologian, 2006.

PORPHYRIOS, SAINT. *Wounded by Love.* Trans. J. Raffin. Evia, Greece: Denise Harvey, 1994.

ROMANIDES, JOHN. *Ancestral Sin.* Trans. G. Gabriel, Ridgewood: Zephyr Publishing, 2002.

SOPHRONY, ARCHIMANDRITE. *Saint Silouan the Athonite.* Trans. R. Edmonds. Essex: Stavropegic Monastery of St. John the Baptist, 1991.

———— *We Shall See Him as He Is.* Trans. R. Edmonds. Essex: Stavropegic Monastery of St. John the Baptist, 1988.

———— *On Prayer.* Trans. R. Edmonds. Essex: Stavropegic Monastery of St. John the Baptist, 1996.

STANILOAE, DUMITRU. *The Experience of God,* Vol. 2. Trans. I. Ionita and R. Barringer. Brookline: Holy Cross Press, 2000.